BANKING
2020

*Transform yourself in the
new era of financial services*

MARK SWAIN

DEDICATION

This book is dedicated to all the great people I worked closely with in financial services, particularly at American Express and ANZ Bank.

I would also like to acknowledge some key friends and supporters in the industry who helped my career be the success that I dreamed of, namely Doug Wood, Robert Staples, Sean Cherrett, Grant Johnstone, Karl Sice, Jarrod Cassidy, Gavin Toole, Shani Marshall, Harry Richmond, David Thomas and Alan Huse.

I would also like to thank the numerous customers who put their trust in me and my sales methodology over the years. Together we created win–win value and worked together to deliver new ideal-state solutions in the world of banking and financial services.

Project management and text design by Michael Hanrahan Publishing
Cover design by Peter Reardon
Images on pages 107 and 110 © Shutterstock

Disclaimer: The material in this publication is of the nature of general comment only and does not represent professional advice. It is not intended to provide specific guidance for particular circumstances and it should not be relied on as the basis for any decision to take action or not take action on any matter which it covers. Readers should obtain professional advice where appropriate, before making any such decision. To the maximum extent permitted by law, the author and publisher disclaim all responsibility and liability to any person, arising directly or indirectly from any person taking or not taking action based on the information in this publication.

CONTENTS

3. How do you grow and transform in this changing environment? 55

4. The future 93

Introduction

The financial services salesperson's guide to industry trends, challenges and opportunities

Why?

The US$2 trillion global commercial banking industry is changing more now than ever before. Established incumbents and nimble fintech entrants are colliding in a fight for customer business and loyalty. All of this is happening in a world of global megatrends and increased information flow, where real-time reviews and immediate customer feedback are handed out on the touch of a smartphone screen.

The race is on to capture and grow market share from demanding customers with heightened expectations. At the same time current revenues have to be grown and existing customers retained.

Many industry employees are worried about future job security as the robots and artificial intelligence start to arrive. Determining what new skills to learn in a rapidly changing financial ecosystem is amongst one of the main employee challenges ahead. Established banks are having to grapple with increased regulatory restrictions and shaky

public perception right at the time new, exciting and customer-friendly options are becoming available.

New ways of creating growth are having to be determined through new products, partnerships, processes and markets.

This book explores the major trends, challenges and opportunities affecting banking and its employees as we move to 2020 and beyond, and importantly provides insights on how you and your business can grow and succeed in the new environment ahead.

With in-depth reviews of the banking strategies of industry participants in all corners of the world from China to the US, India to South America, Asia to the Middle East and Europe to Canada, this book looks into major industry challenges and overlays this with insights on new technology and trends that are going to shape the future growth of financial services.

Banking 2020 gives you a detailed overview of the current global commercial banking industry and importantly ideas and insights to boost your sales and obtain growth in an increasingly competitive and complex environment.

It is a must read for banking and financial services employees working in the industry and information technology and service providers selling to the industry. By reading this book you will be in a stronger position to seize the opportunities ahead, and improve, adapt and transform as we move to Banking 2020 and beyond.

Who?

Mark Swain is a banking business advisor and fintech investor with over 25 years of financial services, payments and strategic sales experience at executive level with companies such as American Express, ANZ Bank and Ingram Micro. His international banking sales career spawned

$10 billion in new transaction values mandated, and over $100 million of profits won in the financial services and technology industries.

During his career he developed the TRANSFORM sales methodology, which helped him consistently deliver sales out-performance and also assisted in launching and growing his own successful tech start-up in the UK.

After a successful career, he now spends the majority of his time providing strategic sales growth advice and employee training to financial services businesses and is involved in a variety of banking start-ups.

Mark is deeply passionate about the combination of customer focus, sales process discipline and innovation in financial services to create opportunities for the unbanked and underprivileged and the businesses that serve them.

His financial services TRANSFORM sales methodology is available at www.nosalesnosleep.com

How?

Banking 2020 starts with a global macro view of the commercial banking industry, including analysis of major revenue pools, key country market analysis and profiles of major competitive participants.

It explores the key challenges facing the industry from cyber-risk to digital transformation, regulation to job losses and more.

It uncovers strategies to grow and transform in the new world of financial services where the customer is making the rules and expectations are for a more customer-focused sales experience.

Finally, it looks towards the future of staffless branches, learning and development for the future bankers, artificial intelligence, robots, open banking and more.

These insights and the analysis reveal challenges and opportunities facing both businesses and employees in the sector.

This book is a must read for all financial sector employees and people doing business with the industry as we move to Banking 2020 and beyond.

1. Understanding the global banking industry

If you and your business are going to thrive in the challenging circumstances facing the banking industry as we move towards 2020 and beyond, you must have a thorough understanding of the current challenges facing the industry. Without this knowledge, you'll be left behind. This chapter will give you a better appreciation of the global commercial banking industry, including the key strategies of major market participants. It will help you better understand current global revenue pools and obtain insights into emerging trends that are driving financial services growth.

The six key megatrends impacting financial services

We are now living in a world that is more connected than ever. In the one minute it will take you to read this page, approximately 187 million emails will have left the outbox, 38 million WhatsApp messages will have been sent, 3.7 million Google searches will have been done and 973,000 Facebook log-ins made.[1] This has had a tremendous impact on businesses all across the globe, and has contributed to the incredible

---

1 www.visualcapitalist.com/internet-minute-2018/

change that dominates the six key megatrends impacting the world of sales and financial services.

These trends are:

1. **Demographic change:** By 2050, 2.1 billion people will be over 60 years old. That's up 320% from 0.5 billion in 1990.

2. **Urbanization:** By 2050 the world's population living in cities is expected to reach 4.9 billion. Currently there are 31 megacities with over 10 million inhabitants; this figure was two in 1970 (New York and Tokyo).

3. **Sustainability:** To support this global expansion, by 2030 50% more energy will be required, 40% more water and 35% more food. Climate change is accelerating, and global temperatures are trending significantly higher.

4. **Technological development:** Internet-connected devices are expected to increase 244% between 2016 and 2020, towards a total of 21 billion.

5. **Globalization:** Global trading has increased by a factor of fifteen since 1960. Developing and emerging economies now account for over 40% of global exports.

6. **Entrepreneurship:** The 'job for life' is no more, and a growing wave of entrepreneurs and freelancers are creating new industries and niche sectors, particularly in financial services.

This is the world we live in now, a world of multitasking, endless choices and non-stop ads across multiple devices. This is the world of disruption and lightning-fast communication. This is the world today's financial services CEOs, VPs, directors, sales managers and sales associates have to generate growth in.

This is the world you must understand.

By the numbers

The global commercial banking industry is large and going through a period of unprecedented change. It employs over 7.2 million people across over 26,000 businesses while generating annual revenues of US$2.16 trillion.[2] Add to this investment banking revenues, insurance, pension funds and other financial service payment providers and the global financial services industry size tops US$14 trillion and over 13 million employees.

The commercial banking industry is approximately the same size as the global oil and gas industry, three times the size of global airlines, and ten times the global market for beer manufacturing (a statistic I found a little surprising given bankers' penchant for a cold brew).

Market size

Commercial banking
US$2 trillion

Global airlines
US$775 billion

Beer
manufacturing
US$225 billion

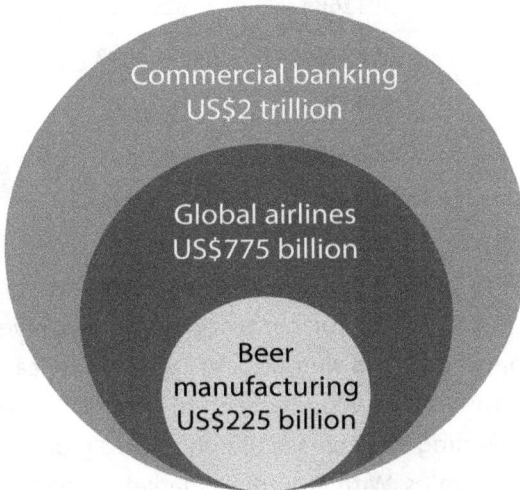

IBISWorld Global Industry Reports

2 IBISWorld Global Commercial Banking Report.

By location

According to research company IBISWorld, revenues from global commercial banking are dominated by the world's two biggest economies, the US and China. Europe has significant banking markets and new developing economies are rapidly increasing financial services revenues and capabilities, including Africa, emerging Asia and the Middle East.

However, the table below shows the size of some countries with the largest financial services industries around the world, by revenue, number of employees and number of businesses.

Country	Annual revenues	Employees	Businesses
Australia	A$146Bn	160,162	34
Canada	C$66Bn	249,489	86
UK	GBP126Bn	326,096	329
US	US$691Bn	2,072,392	78,432
China	US$602Bn	3,612,740	214,833
New Zealand	NZ$24Bn	27,784	24
Germany	E61Bn	161,008	262

Many banks and other financial services businesses are looking to emerging markets to drive further revenue growth, given their large existing customer bases in Europe and North America, which limits the potential to find new customers. In addition, growth-focused businesses are aiming to decrease the unbanked global population in developing economies. With emerging markets expected to be twice the size of developed economies by 2050[3] these new markets offer expansion opportunities for incumbents and new entrants alike.

---

3 United Nations Conference on Trade and Development.

In addition, Asia's middle class alone is expected to grow by over two billion people from 2017 to 2030[4], providing huge growth opportunities for many Asian-focused financial services enterprises.

Where does the money come from?

Traditionally, commercial banking revenues have been generated from interest-related earnings or other non-interest-related fees. Interest revenues come from:

- vehicle loans
- mortgages
- small business loans
- credit cards
- commercial and institutional large corporate loans.

Funds in a banks' deposit current accounts, term deposits and commercial accounts are essentially aggregated and loaned out to bank borrowers at a margin. Wholesale offshore bank borrowing typically covers any difference.

Non-interest revenues are generated from foreign exchange margins, transaction processing fees, loan arrangement fees, late payment fees, commissions and more.

Very broadly speaking, the global revenue mix between consumer-related revenues and business-related revenues is not far off 50/50.

Banks are always looking to raise revenues from new sources, in particular non-interest charging activities which tend to be more stable, predictable and less prone to loan- or deposit-based price competition.

---

4 Global Economy and Development at Brookings, 'The Unprecedented Expansion of the Middle Class' (2017).

Two key divisions

Revenues in commercial banks are usually made up from two key business divisions generally comprising similar product sets:

- retail banking
- institutional banking.

Let's take a look.

Retail banking

Retail banking services typically include a full range of services tailored for individual consumers, such as:

- **Transactional accounts:** Everyday accounts from which individuals can receive payments such as salary and make payments for everything from utility bills to credit card charges. This is the foundation retail product from which most personal financial services cross-selling can occur.

- **Savings accounts:** Interest-paying accounts with withdrawal restrictions and penalties that allow consumers to save for a holiday, house deposit or general purposes.

- **Term deposits:** Putting your money away for between one month and five years to ensure a fixed return on your savings.

- **Credit cards:** To manage day-to-day purchases on extended terms for on- and off-line purchases in popular categories such as groceries, travel, online shopping and more.

- **Foreign exchange:** Comprises buying and selling of foreign currencies for holidays and international money transfers for larger overseas purchases.

- **Home loans:** Provides long-term funding to buy a first home, next home or investment property through provision of secured mortgages.

- **Personal loans:** Covers secured car loans and other personal loans.

- **Private banking:** Services offered to high-wealth clients from a private client manager across investment services including real estate and investments. Also includes asset protection and insurance.

- **Share trading:** Providing equities trading capabilities in domestic and sometimes international shares.

Institutional banking

The other half of the global revenue pool is generated through the provision of banking services to businesses, governments and institutional clients. This is the area I spent the majority of my career working in. Institutional banking is a specialized division within a bank that offers a comprehensive suite of products and services for corporate, government and large business clients locally and abroad. The following key product components typically make up the majority of institutional earnings:

- **Transaction banking:** Managing business payables and receivables efficiently through working capital account(s), while ensuring safe and efficient management of funds. This is the foundational institutional product providing day-to-day bank client interaction from which additional product and service cross-selling can occur.

- **Markets:** Sales and trading teams providing a complete range of financial markets products such as foreign exchange, commodities, interest rate risk, fixed income, investment products, capital markets and equity derivatives.

- **Loans:** Usually incorporating syndicated loans, project finance, acquisition finance and structured export finance.

- **Trade:** Trade finance loans, structured trade finance, and financial and performance guarantees to support businesses trading internationally and managing large projects onshore and offshore.

- **Commercial cards:** Corporate and purchasing cards to manage day-to-day business expenses at home and abroad.

- **Merchant solutions:** A range of physical off- and on-line technologies to accept credit and debit card payments from customers.

- **Supply chain finance:** Supply chain finance allows a supplier to sell its invoices to a bank at a discount as soon as they are approved by the buyer. This allows the buyer to pay later and the supplier to secure its money earlier. Instead of relying on the creditworthiness of the supplier, the bank deals with the buyer – usually a less risky prospect.

As we can see, there are myriad different banking and financial product solutions that make up the US$2 trillion global commercial banking revenue pool. These revenues are not only spread across different products but among different customer profiles, many of which often have different underlying needs.

Banking and the global economy

A healthy global economy drives demand for commercial banking services, and after a sharp decline in lending and transaction volumes after the Global Financial Crisis (GFC) caused by rising unemployment, asset value reductions to both property and shares, and declining wages, the industry is now experiencing steady growth again.

Following the well-publicized bailouts of financial institutions during the GFC – including Royal Bank of Scotland, Lloyds Bank, Fannie Mae,

Freddie Mac, AIG, Bank of America and Citigroup – there has been increased regulatory requirements around banks to hold increased capital and liquidity, essentially to hold higher levels of balances for security in downturns and to clearly segment proprietary trading activities to a maximum of 3% of a bank's total core capital (through the 'Volcker rule').

With an ecosystem spread across the world, but not yet a global ecosystem, the industry is returning from the shocks of the GFC with a new range of challenges and opportunities for industry players and employed participants.

Commercial banking is also a large driver of the global economy, not only from an employment and lending perspective but also from the large amounts the industry spends in its own financial supply chain in areas such as information technology and real estate.

With 7.2 million people working in commercial banks around the world and a figure of 16 million within the wider financial services industry globally according to LinkedIn, it will be critical for staff to adapt and change to a rapidly changing industry and global landscape.

Banking and technology

There is little doubt that automation and technology advancements in the areas of artificial intelligence (AI) and machine learning will over time have a big impact on the face of financial services employment. New technologies will definitely reshape the face of financial services, just as the automatic teller machines (ATMs) allowed branch staff to move from transactional activities to serving customers in the 1980s and 1990s.

As technology pervades all industries the banking workforce of the future will need to be more digitally savvy, more mobile, and may move to contract-based roles as the freelancer economy gathers momentum.

It is also highly likely that people working in bank branches and corporate centers now will soon be working alongside digital colleagues as early as 2019. Expect to be interacting with something like this at a bank branch or corporate center near you soon.

Emerging entrants

Based on approximately US$1 trillion in global retail banking revenues and US$1 trillion in global institutional banking revenues, it's no surprise that not only is business hotly contested in major markets among established incumbents but new entrants with niche solutions are starting to chip away at the large banks' traditionally safe-haven revenue streams.

Emerging players looking to disrupt the current commercial banking landscape with new propositions include:

- **Neobanks:** These are new digitally focused banks largely being built from the ground up without any historical legacy infrastructure. The UK has Atom Bank, Monzo and Starling Bank to name a few, Australia has Xinja, Volt and 86 400, Germany has N26, Poland has mBank and the US has Chime, Simple and GoBank. In other markets around the world neobanks are setting up in increasing numbers and at increasing speed.

- **Lending:** New ways of borrowing are emerging through online peer-to-peer lending marketplaces connecting people with money to the people needing it. Zopa, Prosper, RateSetter and Lending Club are a few such examples.

- **Payments:** Platform-based foreign exchange providers offering competitive exchange transfers on a simple platform are rapidly

emerging. Transferwise in the UK is one such example, as are Azimo and CurrencyFair.

If we consider that an established bank such as JP Morgan processes around US$5 trillion in international wholesale payment flows on a daily basis, it's not hard to see why taking even a small share of this is of big appeal to nimble new entrants.

Interestingly, Ernst & Young's recent fintech Adoption Index[5] highlights that 'consumers are drawn to fintech services because propositions are simpler, more convenient, more transparent and more readily personalized'. This is especially the case in what have been traditionally profitable parts of the banking value chain. Adoption of fintech as providers of money transfer and payment services rose from 18% in 2015 to 50% in 2017, with 65%[6] of consumers anticipating they would use such services at some point in future.

- **Digital wallets:** Smartphone-based payments bypassing physical card use from providers such as Paytm, Paypal, Alipay and Amazon are experiencing high growth and adoption. Citibank have launched Citi Pay in the US, a new omnichannel digital wallet as well as mobile wallets in several Asian markets.

- **Merchant innovation:** With the rapid growth of card-based payments, tap and go transactions and mobile wallets, new emerging merchant processors and aggregators are appearing in cafés and online. Square, Stripe, Adyen and Klarna are a few examples with new innovative customer-centric tailored propositions.

As CEO of JP Morgan Jamie Dimon recently wrote in a letter to share-holders about start-ups: 'When I go to Silicon Valley, they all want to eat

---

5 and 6 EY FinTech Adoption Index 2017.

our lunch, every single one of them is going to try and a lot of them will succeed.'

With that said, large incumbent commercial banks have significant customer bases in many markets and are highly regulated. In Australia where I live, banks are regulated by APRA (the Australian Prudential Regulation Authority) which sets regulations industry operators should comply with and determines minimum capital adequacy requirements. The situation is similar in most other markets around the world.

While many governments are encouraging fintech innovation and welcome increased competition in the industry, financial regulation (as we delve into later) and obtaining licenses to access markets is becoming the dividing line for how far and fast many emerging market participants and disruptors can enter the industry.

For example, in Australia, offering full banking services is conditional upon getting a banking license through APRA. Even obtaining a Restricted Authorised Deposit Institution license (RADI) to be able to take smaller customer deposits involves significant investment in engaging legal advisors, accountants and consultants in assisting with the application. Invariably a RADI-type license allows start-up banks to operate under restricted conditions for a period of time before being validated for the full process of acquiring a full banking license. Other licenses are also required to offer products such as mortgages, where an Australian Credit License (ACL) is required.

Given the historical complexity, significant investment and time required to obtain regulatory and financial approvals to offer banking services in most countries, the industry is often dominated by three or four key players in each market.

Industry statistics

The section that follows and the appendix look at the strategies of major banks in all corners of the world. It is designed to give you an idea of key global emerging themes and competitive strategies.

United States

As an established global financial center the US has the largest commercial banking market in the world at US$691 billion, closely followed by China.

Bank of America, JP Morgan, Citigroup and Wells Fargo are the dominant big four providers in this large market, accounting for over US$300 billion of industry revenues.

In total there are over 5,000 Federal Deposit Insurance Corporation (FDIC) insured banks in America made up from commercial banks, thrifts (savings and loans associations), credit unions (cooperative financial institutions) and online banks.

Some 10 years after the Global Financial Crisis, American banks are recovering from the write offs and losses to build more steady growth in a strengthening domestic and global economy.

Bank	Total revenue (billion)	Strategy	Focus	Interesting consideration	Interesting challenge
Bank of America	US$91.2	US-centered bank focused on individual, commercial and institutional customers.	Key focus on responsible growth through better serving of customers and better managing risks.	Working out ways to maximize opportunities from the US corporate tax acts following lowering of the corporate tax rate from 35% to 21%.	Focusing on enhanced digital capabilities across 4,500 financial center branches.
JP Morgan	US$111.5	Strong focus on consumer banking, asset and wealth management, commercial banking and large corporate and investment banking.	Big focus on organic growth from existing customers.	Renewed focus on client onboarding process across the bank. Balancing roughly 80% US – 20% global revenue split.	Managing investments in cyber-security to protect clients from fraud and cyber-risks.
Citibank	US$72.9	Serving two core franchises of consumer banking and institutional clients with focus.	Maximizing value from globally integrated business model.	Managing global network with physical locations in 98 countries.	Finding ways to globally expand digital capabilities.
Wells Fargo	US$86.4	Strong home loan and small business lending focus in North America.	Improving sales practises following government review of historical sales approach.	Working with Federal Reserve to improve the board's governance, compliance and operational risk.	Introducing a streamlined vision, values and goals across the organisation.

China

China has expanded significantly in recent years as the country transitions from a manufacturing and export-oriented focus to a more domestic service- and consumption-focused economy. The world's second-largest economy is expected to have the largest global commercial banking industry by 2020. According to IBISWorld the current Chinese commercial banking industry is worth over US$600 billion in revenues. Massive infrastructure projects such as the impressive 'Belt and Road' initiative to connect east with west are likely to generate further growth in this burgeoning economy.

Agricultural Bank of China, Bank of China, Bank of Communication, China Construction Bank and China Merchants Bank are the dominant providers in this market, accounting for over 50% market share. We should not however overlook the progress of Jack Ma's Alibaba Group and new market entrants like fintech CreditEase, who have gone from zero to 35,000 staff in five years. Five of the top 10 fintech businesses globally are Chinese, with this large market offering significant growth opportunities for innovative start-ups and well-recognized expansionary global offshore players. In addition, China's entry into the World Trade Organization (WTO) is expected to further propel market size and scale.

Chinese consumers traveling and businesses expanding outside of their home market also offer significant growth opportunities, as demonstrated by the huge numbers of Chinese tourists using new payment products when traveling overseas.

The big banks in China are state-owned commercial banks and among the largest banks in the world. In addition to the big five Chinese banks there are 145 city commercial banks, around 2,000 small-sized rural banks and over 40 locally incorporated foreign banks.

Bank	Total revenue (billion)	Strategy	Focus	Interesting consideration	Interesting challenge
Agricultural Bank of China	RMB542 (US$79.95)	Specialists in providing financing to China's agricultural sector through offering wholesale and retail banking services.	Seizing opportunities arising from rural revitalization strategy.	Debt support for long-term national projects such as Yangtze River Economic zone, Beijing-Tianjin economic region and construction of the new Xiong'an area.	Helping China transition from a rapid growth phase to a stage of high-quality development. This will require transformation and development.
Bank of China	RMB483.7 (US$71.35)	Specialists in foreign exchange transactions and trade finance.	US$100 billion in approved credit lines for countries along the Belt and Road project.	Long-term plan by 2050 to become a 'financial treasure' of a great modern socialist country, and serve as a paragon of the global financial industry.	Supporting the country's growing modernization.
Industrial and Commercial Bank of China	RMB726.5 (US$107.17)	Large foreign exchange and bank clearing focus.	Active support of small and micro businesses, agriculture, rural areas and rural residents.	The world's largest bank measured by assets focused on supporting China's progress and providing real economy support.	Macro policies to help combat material risks, poverty and pollution.

Bank	Total revenue (billion)	Strategy	Focus	Interesting consideration	Interesting challenge
China Construction Bank	RMB622 (US$91.75)	Specializes in medium to long-term credit for specialized projects such as infrastructure and urban housing development.	Supporting middle-market small business expansion.	Helping develop Guangdong–Hong Kong–Macau Bay Area.	Effectively managing a network of 14,985 branches.
Alibaba	RMB250 (US$36.88)	Get business ready for five new trends of the future: New Retail, New Manufacturing, New Finance, New Technology and New Resources.	Expansion into FMCG (fast-moving consumer goods).	Improving technological infrastructure, cloud computing capabilities and investing in digital media and entertainment.	Maintain position as largest retail commerce business in the world.

Asia

With the ASEAN (Association of South East Asian Nations) population soon expected to hit 717 million people from a 2015 total of 633 million, these markets offer exciting growth opportunities for banks and financial service providers expanding offshore. Many economies are growing GDP at 6% or above, and with a rising middle class migrating from manufacturing to service-based economies the area offers a wealth of opportunities. Many banks in the region are focusing heavily on digital strategies to capture the hearts and minds of millennial consumers and expanding domestic businesses.

Bank	Total revenue (billion)	Strategy	Focus	Interesting consideration	Interesting challenge
DBS Group Singapore	SGD11.9 billion income (~US$8.70 billion)	Strong focus on digital transformation and making banking joyful.	Focus on fast-growing populous emerging markets such as Indonesia, India and China.	Carefully managing lending practise to environmental impact industries such as Palm Oil and Resources.	Embedding a start-up culture across the organisation.
MayBank Malaysia	Revenue RM45.58 billion (~US$10.97 billion)	Maximizing ASEAN growth potential and meeting evolving customer needs, particularly in core markets of Malaysia, Singapore and Indonesia.	Heavy focus on insurance and Islamic finance.	Investing in managing increased threats from cyber-security globally.	Embedding MayBank's GO Ahead upskilling of workforce.
Siam Commercial Bank Thailand	Revenues THB136.21 billion (~US$4.15 billion)	Going upside-down strategy to lean the bank, digitally acquire, provide high-margin lending, develop data capabilities and a platform business model.	Focusing on the bank's three core businesses: business lending, consumer lending and wealth management.	Supporting Thailand's transition to a cashless society in line with the government's national e-payment program.	Managing likely Thai baht appreciation and low agricultural prices due to excess supply.

Bank	Total revenue (billion)	Strategy	Focus	Interesting consideration	Interesting challenge
Bank Mandiri Indonesia	Revenue Rp78.1 trillion (~US$5.47 billion)	Continue strong relationships and focus on large wholesale institutional customers. Accelerate middle-income class customer growth.	Accelerate growth segments, integrate the group and deepen client relationships.	Maintain strong growth in market micro finance.	Manage against aggressive market competitiveness.
BDO Unibank Philippines	Revenue P129. billion (~US$2.45 billion)	Building diversified earnings stream across products, creating operational leverage from network and prudently managing balance sheet.	Expansion into microfinance and mid-sized enterprises.	Effectively managing a nationwide branch network of some 1,180 strong.	Managing additional regulatory measures introduced in 2017.
Mitsubishi UFJ Financial Group Japan	Revenue Yen5194 billion (~US$46.7 billion)	Focus on exceeding expectations of customer, providing reliable and consistent support and strengthening global presence.	Focus on Japanese retail, corporate, global banking and markets, and investor services/asset management.	Implement digital transformation initiatives in a new world where big techs and digital players now participate.	Managing ultra-low interest rate environment.

It is interesting when reviewing the above analysis and the appendix data how in many markets it is not unusual for the top four or five banks to hold up to 80% total market share.

The 'big four' has become a popular household term in many countries where the banking industry is largely dominated by four institutions. Countries where a big four dominate are wide ranging, and include markets such as Australia, Austria, Belgium, Brazil, Canada (big five), China, France, India, Ireland, Italy, Japan, Netherlands, Nigeria, Pakistan, Philippines, Portugal, Singapore (big three), South Africa, South Korea, Spain, Sweden, Taiwan, Thailand, UK, US and Vietnam.

The key question is, can it stay this way? And how do these businesses plan for growth in a fast-moving competitive landscape where nearly every bank has a goal to be the best digital provider? We will discuss growth opportunities and the future in more detail in chapters three and four.

The rapid growth of electronic payments

One such area of fantastic growth potential in financial services is the move away from cash to card-based and electronic payments. Visa alone in its recent financial year processed US$11 trillion in card volumes across 3.3 billion cards, driven by over 180 billion transactions.

However, according to Visa an estimated two billion people worldwide still lack access to formal financial services, with last year US$17 trillion still transacted in cash and checks globally in the consumer-to-business channel. This is a tremendous opportunity for global financial services expansion and social impact.

Mastercard estimates in its recent annual report that the total addressable card payment flows across business to business (B2B), person to

person (P2P) and business to consumer (B2C) is as high as US$225 trillion, an astounding number I'm sure you will agree. Cash, checks and slower-batch EFT or ACH payments currently make up 90% of this significant market opportunity. US$120 trillion of this is B2B payment flows, of which US$100 trillion is directly related to accounts payable volumes.

American Express are also not missing out on the move from cash to electronic card-based payments, with worldwide card spending recently increasing 5% to US$1.1 trillion.

Digital payments platform provider PayPal is a great example of a relatively new entrant into the financial ecosystem adopting new technologies and expansion into new markets of cashless payments to achieve high growth rates.

According to PayPal's recent annual report, person to person (P2P) payment volume grew 50% on the prior year period. Venmo, the company's social payments platform, processed US$10.4 billion in payment volume in the fourth quarter alone, an increase of 86% year over year. In addition, PayPal have also announced the launch of domestic operations in India, with merchants able to process both local and global payments through their platform. The company is currently expecting around 15% to 17% growth, showing how financial services providers offering good customer solutions combined with entry into emerging markets can be a recipe for top-line revenue growth.

Ant Financial – the banking subsidiary of Alibaba – recently enabled some merchants near Everest Base Camp with a QR code to allow commerce and financial progress in one of the world's most remote locations. There is no doubt the world of cashless payments is rapidly evolving and innovatively touching merchants and consumers in brand new geographies and locations.

* * *

As you can see, and as I'm sure you already know, banking and financial services is a huge industry with a multitude of different products. Established incumbents are defending market share and nimble entrants are chipping away at previously predictable revenue streams.

In the next chapter I'm going to highlight some of the challenges established market participants in commercial banking and financial services and new entrants alike are encountering, before explaining in chapter three ideas for growth as we move towards 2020 and beyond.

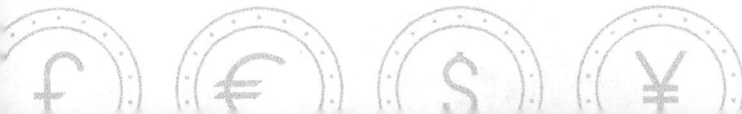

2. Industry challenges

Set out in this chapter are some of the key challenges financial services industry employees and businesses need to be aware of as we emerge from the Global Financial Crisis into the information age.

In this chapter I have drawn on my insights and experience from over 20 years of client meetings in the industry, as well as research on leading and emerging banks and financial service and technology providers from all regions of the world. Layered on top of this is recent learnings from attending technology and banking conferences all around the world.

My aim is to distil the industry challenges into dominant key themes that banks and financial service providers face moving forward. These are topics all participants in the industry need to be acutely aware of to best prepare for a changing industry outlook and to seize the significant growth opportunities ahead.

Growing competition from within the industry

Despite recent record global profits, the internal competition within the financial services industry is aggressive and unrelenting. I can testify

to this from many years spent in the Australian and Asian markets structuring financial solutions and managing competitive transaction banking pitches, presentations and RFPs (request for proposals) for large domestic and multinational corporations.

From a global perspective, at a very high level the customer has a wide range of choice in banking and payment providers, all of which can do a reasonable job providing the core banking functionality required. Customers are invariably looking for a great combination of price, platform, insights, service, security and reliability, with service providers under more pressure than ever to find innovative new ways to differentiate themselves from the competition.

Both business and consumer customers are expecting more, as service experiences from outside the industry in exclusive retail, fintech and online raise expectations and raise the bar.

In addition, aggressive competition from local incumbents in key regions of Asia, Europe, North America and many other global markets is putting pressure on fees and margins in a low-interest-rate environment.

Every bank seems to have the same goal of delivering the best digital banking application and streamlining processes for improved customer service and efficiency savings. According to Ernst & Young, 85% of banks globally are pursuing digital transformation as a business priority for 2018/19. In reality, not every provider can achieve this and be the number one in any given market. Having the leading offering and best service in the eyes of the customer will require much more moving forward than a user-friendly mobile app and online chatbot. Successful businesses in the sector and successful sales and relationship teams will need to adapt to the challenges that follow and formulate a clear and consistent plan for growth.

In chapter one, I explained the size of the global commercial banking market and highlighted some of the key market players that dominate

a large proportion of this US$2 trillion global business. Over the next two to three years, having a customer-obsessed mindset will be crucial to these financial services providers maintaining strong positions, something that is easy to say but very hard to do.

Banks are going to have to get much better at delivering real value in the eyes of the customer, which facilitates cross-selling of different solutions. The days of being reliant largely on mortgages and transactional accounts are over, as nimble competitors start breaking away components of the traditional banking value chain. Banks will need to find ways to better package combined value through complete insights rather than being too reliant on vanilla loans, deposit accounts and mortgage sales.

Industry competition is expected to increase over the next five years with an accessible, yet focused distribution network, strong digital offering, fast transaction execution, excellent service and a strong, secure reputation all important considerations.

Often, as previously mentioned, internal market competition is very aggressive among three or four key dominant market providers, but now there is also stiff competition from tier-two banks, building societies, credit unions, digital-only offerings, savings banks and specialist card issuers and acquirers. Merchant banks, investment banks and private equity firms also offer strong additional competition in the institutional market.

For example, Lloyds Bank in the UK has mentioned how the landscape continues to evolve and the domestic incumbents are intensifying their focus in that market. FirstRand Bank in South Africa is seeing intensifying competition from non-traditional disruptors and insurance market entrants. In Australia, the big four ANZ, CBA, NAB and Westpac are competing heavily to increase mortgage market share and their

share of the small business customer base. Second-tier banks and new digital entrants are also snapping at their heels.

Singapore and Hong Kong as regional financial centers where many multinational regional treasury centers are located are well known for intense competition on debt and cash management mandates. Even markets such as South Korea are seeing intense competition spread across over 100 banks, comprising national commercial banks, regional banks, foreign banks and mutual savings banks.

Throw on top of this a government push to expand fintech adoption in many countries and you can see how an already high level of internal industry competition is about to get a whole lot tougher.

Huge competition from outside the industry

Incumbent providers that do not effectively respond and adapt to changing customer requirements in fast, responsive, customer-focused ways will lose market share, as has been seen in many other industries such as film (Kodak), newspapers, and entertainment (Blockbuster).

The banking and finance industry is undergoing significant change that is altering the business model from what we have historically known. Every day new competitors, fintech entrants and hungry entrepreneurs are seeking new ways to disrupt the world of financial services. Businesses light in operation, low on costs and versatile in service are offering new and flexible alternatives to customers. Payments, lending, money transfers, investments and insurance are all areas seeing new competitive threats from outside the traditional banking industry. New entrants are using the latest technologies, often to target small, profitable niche segments.

TransferWise, who have developed an API-based money transfer system, are a great example of a participant entering from outside

the industry to claim market share. (API stands for application programming interfaces.) A start up that set up in 2011 is now processing GBP2 billion in payments per month. In addition, technology giants such as Apple, Facebook and Google are driving up disintermediation risk and posing a new external competitive threat to the financial services sector. These enterprises are cash rich and have large customer bases, strong brand loyalty and access to copious amounts of customer data which they manage very efficiently.

Fintech businesses are accelerating at a rapid pace, with certain markets such as China making significant progress. Alipay is one such example, processing over 250,000 transactions per second at times during 2018 across multiple locations. To put this into perspective, Visa processes an average of 500 million transactions every day.

Increasing customer expectations

As someone who manages a property through the great property-connecting platform Airbnb, I get to see firsthand how customers' expectations are rapidly changing.

Interested guests can specifically search for the type of property they want to stay at and read detailed reviews of guests who have stayed. Guests can search for the accommodation experience they feel will specifically meet their needs, instead of the more general offering of a central business district hotel. Guests often expect to check in early or check out late for no extra charge (something I am flexible on to deliver great customer experience whenever possible). Guests get charged automatically in one click without any cumbersome process of keying in card details each booking. They get a seamless payment experience combined with a different travel experience. And it's not unusual for digital-friendly millennial guests to book an apartment at 6 pm to check in at 7 pm that evening.

Customer experiences in this world of booking accommodation, travel and buying online are now setting customer expectations for the world of banking and financial services. Customers are expecting faster, on-demand, personal service and unique experiences. Many financial service providers are struggling to adjust fast enough to these changing demands.

Businesses and individuals now have to be able to act in a real-time market where five-star reviews or harsh criticism are handed out over social media by customers immediately. These customers' demands will not subside but only increase, and when companies fail to deliver to meet heightened customer expectations, customers will more readily take flight and go elsewhere. Banking won't be excluded from these changes.

Job losses

My better half Jessica, who works in a bank branch around 10 kilometers from where we live in Sydney, helps customers with their day-to-day banking needs. She helps people set up new accounts, arranges credit cards for new customers, provides loan guidance, helps new businesses set up facilities and provides advice on mortgages. She also loves helping set up kids with their first savings accounts.

Customers like the personal service that Jessica delivers, and quite often they bring her chocolates, other small tokens of appreciation, and even flowers for the outstanding customer service she delivers. Customers enjoy dealing with a real person who is customer focused, not pushy and who helps them achieve their financial goals and also helps the community. The branch is in a high-foot-traffic shopping mall, has a welcoming, open-plan, relaxed layout, and is always vibrant and busy with business booming due to happy customers. Customers say they feel part of a family dealing with Jessica and the happy team at the branch.

But Jessica recently received news from head office that the branch was closing in two months. She will be supported in finding a new role in the group or offered redundancy.

I share this example because it's a common theme playing out in bank branches and discussions around family dining tables currently; it's a stark reality of the financial services landscape we work in and it highlights to me how we need a plan B to survive and thrive in the industry.

You know how humans tend to overdo things from time to time, get caught up in excitement, euphoria and promises of great riches or cost savings? I'm thinking the dotcom technology boom, the subprime housing run up and subsequent meltdown, and more recently the overzealous purchasing of Bitcoin and other crypto-currencies from many people seeking quick returns but experiencing quite the opposite come sale time. Personally, I believe digital transformation and the branch scale-back is going to be one such area where banks overdo things. I believe many banks will eliminate too many staff and try to automate too much, given a relentless focus on what the competition and industry are doing rather than focusing squarely on the customer.

Now, I'm not saying bank digital transformation is not important – it's crucially important. But so is providing caring, customer-focused staff in select prime locations to help people face to face to manage the important and sensitive topic of their money.

In the example of Jess above, I cannot comprehend why any business would close a booming branch in a prime location, where customers are delighted and continually being serviced and sold to. If it was a café, a bicycle repair shop or a florist, would they shut up shop?

Interestingly, on my last visit to a branch in the UK in Northampton, I was talking to a gentleman in the queue who was about 60 or 65. He was fit and healthy looking, with probably 25 years to live. His town

center branch had closed, and the nearest one offered was in Leicester, 61 kilometers away.

What did he do? He closed his account and moved it to a bank with a branch and service nearby. That business has been lost forever, and I would not be at all surprised if he had over GBP250,000 on deposit with that bank.

Digital transformation

It will be important as the digital transformation agenda unfolds that banks move at a pace their customers are comfortable with, and that they also allow customers to choose how they want to interact with their bank. While digital banking is a great step forward and banks are right to embrace and encourage online and mobile banking, face-to-face interaction will always be an important way for people to communicate about money. Banks that have a strong complement of digital and human capabilities are likely to succeed moving forward as they will be meeting the distinct needs of different customer profiles.

The emerging reality appears to be that many banks will use digital transformation to radically resize and reshape workforces and take costs out of business models, and having other options will be important for many financial services employees. (In chapter three I talk in more detail about having a human-centered, empathetic, creative sales process that cannot be easily automated, and give guidance on new skills to learn in chapter four to maintain relevance in the industry.)

In both developing and emerging markets, online and mobile banking technologies are reducing the need for teller staff and physical bank branches. Platforms are replacing branches and allowing customers to access their accounts anywhere at any time and providing the freedom to pay bills and transfer funds when it best suits the customer.

Commercial banks in many developed markets are starting to down-size branch networks in response to this new digitally focused agenda. Since the Global Financial Crisis, Barclays in the UK has gone under one of the biggest bank transformations ever and shed a stunning 80,000 jobs.

Nordea, the Scandinavian banking provider, has indicated that due to digital technologies, robotics and artificial intelligence, at least 4,000 fewer employees and 2,000 fewer consultants will be required over the next few years. Bank Hapoalim of Israel in the five years to 2017 have lost 455 staff (down 19%) and have 17% fewer branches.

ANZ Bank of Australia's 2018 annual review indicates that full-time staff members have reduced to 39,924 as at September 2018, compared to 50,152 in September 2015. This is a reduction of 10,228 staff in a three-year period, or 20.5%.

Lloyds Bank of the UK has shed 30,000 jobs since 2011. In June 2018 Lloyds said it would cut another 450 roles as part of moves to increase productivity and respond to 'changes in consumer behavior'. These changes are on top of 1,230 job cuts announced in April 2018 and 930 in February 2018.

Deutsche Bank, Germany's largest bank by total lending, announced in May 2018 7,000 jobs will be lost globally as it overhauls its investment banking operations and focuses on cost reductions.

Media reports throughout Japan have indicated recently that Japanese banks are expected to reduce jobs by up to 33,000 positions over the next decade due to digital downsizing.

Whether banks overdo the digital staffing cutbacks or not, be sure to figure out a plan B – and read chapter three to remain relevant in the industry.

Cyber-risk

'Cyber-crime is costing UK firms billions and has the potential to seriously disrupt our economy and wider society.'
Dan Crisp, Director (Interim) Technology and Digital Policy, UK Finance

We have all heard about some of the major cyber-attacks over the last couple of years:

- Credit bureau Equifax was penetrated by cyber-criminals between May and July 2017, who stole the personal data of 146 million people, including 146 million dates of birth, 146 million US social security numbers, 99 million addresses and 209,000 payment card numbers and expiration dates.

- In November 2017 former CEO of Yahoo Marissa Mayer told congress up to 1 billion Yahoo accounts had been hacked.

- The Cambridge Analytica and Facebook data issue hit the global headlines with the congressional testimony held in April 2018.

- In 2016, hackers stole the data of 57 million Uber customers.

And that's just a few examples.

Cyber-risk and attacks are only expected to accelerate, with cloud-based businesses holding massive amounts of data for large companies and financial institutions holding significant funds being obvious targets. Service providers that host email and photo library storage are other candidates for attack.

The WannaCry ransomware attack that struck the UK NHS Health service in 2017 prevented workers from accessing their computers and delayed vital medical procedures. Nissan Motor Manufacturing, Telefónica, FedEx, Deutsche Bahn and other multinational companies' operations were also affected.

Cyber-risk is probably the biggest single risk to the financial services and commercial banking industry, with cyber-criminals fully aware of the massive amounts of money swirling through the ecosystem. In fact, cyber-crime is a massive challenge to many industries, including core utility providers, transport systems and governments themselves. With new technologies developing rapidly alongside organized crime, nation state attacks and cyber-fraud, protecting customers' transactions, data and privacy will become of utmost concern.

Banks and financial institutions are likely to be one of the most heavily targeted sectors by cyber-criminals seeking to hack into the accounts of customers or slow down online banking operations. Jamie Dimon, CEO of JP Morgan, eloquently describes the situation in the company's recent annual report:

> We cannot do enough as a country when it comes to cyber-security. I cannot overemphasize the importance of cyber-security in America. This is a critical issue, not just for financial companies but also for utilities, technology companies, electrical grids and others. It is an arms race, and we need to do whatever we can to protect the United States of America.

I was amazed at a recent financial services conference in Singapore when Ralph Echemendia, CEO of Seguru and self-branded 'ethical hacker', took to the stage and started pulling up people's saved passwords live from Google in front of the 3,000 strong audience, who quite rightly gasped and shook their heads. Ralph explained how cyber-fraud is likely to dramatically grow from a current US$300 million annually in 2017 to up to an annual US$1 trillion in the next few years. Amazingly, he mentioned it takes on average 22 days to detect fraud when it occurs. With connected devices exploding up to 50 billion in number by 2020, banks will have to invest significant amounts to stem and contain this major ecosystem challenge.

Finding the perpetrators of cyber-crime often involves collaboration across multiple entities and geographies. Many of the UK's biggest banks were targeted in 2017, with in excess of 4 million distributed denial of service (DDOS) email attacks, where high volumes of internet traffic are launched at target computers and companies to disable them. The investigation was led by the National Crime Agency and the Dutch National Police, and involved authorities in five countries including Netherlands, Serbia, Croatia, Canada and UK. Additional support was provided by Police Scotland and Europol to target six members of the crime group behind webstresser.org.

And there have been many more such attacks. Bank of Montreal and Canadian Imperial Bank of Commerce revealed in May 2018 that cyber-attackers had possibly stolen the data of over 50,000 customers in what appeared to be the first significant assault on financial institutions in the country.

The Bank of Chile announced in June 2018 hackers had siphoned off US$10 million of its funds, mainly to Hong Kong.

In Mexico in May 2018 cyber-thieves used phantom orders and fake accounts to steal hundreds of millions of Mexican pesos from the country's banks, including Banorte.

In February 2016 the first ever central bank cyber-attack took place with the Bangladesh Bank. Instructions to fraudulently withdraw US$1 billion from the account of Bangladesh Bank held at the Federal Reserve Bank of New York were issued via the SWIFT payment network. Five transactions issued by security hackers worth $101 million succeeded, with US$20 million traced to Sri Lanka and US$81 million to the Philippines. It was later identified that Dridex malware was used for the attack.

Information security and cyber-security will be one of the highest strategic priorities for banks' boards and management teams moving

forward, and will sit squarely alongside their digital transformation agendas at board level. Bank security and privacy teams are going to need to know exactly who is accessing what at all times, and will need to combine smart artificial intelligence with human creative thinking to minimize fraudulent and cyber-risk activities.

Banks will never be one step in front of the cyber-criminals, but they sure as hell need to be quickly one step behind to intercept their damaging efforts. Having strong cyber-security capabilities and fraud-prevention activities will over time become a stronger part of a financial service provider's value proposition. Many banks are investing heavily in cyber-security, as demonstrated by JP Morgan's acquisition of Brighterion, Inc., a software consulting company specializing in artificial intelligence that enhances the company's internal networks, enhances the product suite, and builds the next generation of solutions to tackle fraud and cyber-security threats. And Ant Financial of China have invested in a huge NASA-style artificial intelligence–based center to monitor fraud, cyber-risks and money laundering in real time.

Cyber-security will represent a big chunk of the burgeoning information technology budget increases banks will be spending into the early 2020s. Consumers and businesses themselves are likely to be asking more questions about how their information is stored, shared and protected as open banking and the cyber-crime challenge gather momentum globally. The consumer voice will grow much louder over the coming years, asking banks, 'Do you guarantee to protect my funds and data?'

Regulation

Banking regulation is a form of government regulation that subjects banks to certain requirements, restrictions and guidelines designed to create market transparency between banking institutions and the

individuals and corporations with whom they conduct business and to provide protection for consumers, among other things.

Since the 2008 financial crisis, government regulators across the world have been working to reduce risks in the global commercial banking industry. With financial regulation becoming stricter, the financial industry is now under more pressure to meet regulatory requirements.

One could argue that too much regulation has been introduced since the financial crisis, given regulatory burdens generate significant restrictions and high compliance costs for global commercial banks. Managing strict and multi-layered new regulations will act as a key challenge for the industry moving towards 2020 and beyond. The focus on regulation is creating a complex environment for commercial banks and financial service providers as national governments look to take more control.

Dodd-Frank

New regulations around the world have increased the amount of capital banks must have in their reserves, and in markets like the US the Dodd-Frank reform limits the range of activities commercial banks can perform.

The *Dodd-Frank Wall Street Reform and Consumer Protection Act* was signed into US law in July 2010, and essentially places regulation of the financial industry in the hands of the government. Dodd-Frank changed the regulatory and compliance landscape for industry participants in significant ways.

Ultimately the Act was designed to promote financial stability in the US following the Global Financial Crisis, by improving accountability and subjecting banks to a number of regulations, including the possibility of being broken up if any of them are determined to be 'too big to fail'. In addition, Dodd-Frank was designed to protect the American

taxpayer by ending bailouts, and to protect consumers from abusive financial services practises.

Basel III

Basel III is intended to strengthen bank capital requirements by increasing liquidity and decreasing bank leverage. This global capital framework requires financial institutions to hold more capital and a higher quality of capital to protect customers and better absorb losses from shocks that could emanate from anywhere.

A clear lesson from the Global Financial Crisis was that regulatory capital requirements across banks was too low and leverage far too high. Prior to 2010, banks were allowed to increase leverage to the highest ever levels, increasing risk in the financial system. When the Global Financial Crisis hit, subsequent government support resulted in taxpayer-funded bailouts around the world.

Ultimately Basel III significantly increases global financial security and stability through banks needing to hold common equity capital of at least 7% of their risk-based assets, compared to 2% prior to the Global Financial Crisis. Banks must now hold onto more reserves and implement safeguards against issuing risky loans. Basel III ultimately impacts a bank's ability to make loans and may cause some tightening of global credit. Basel III also involves stress-testing to examine a bank's ability to withstand a range of economic shocks and market dislocation.

In my home market Australia, new regulation and policy demands driven by APRA, ASIC, AUSTRAC, ACCC and the Financial Services Royal Commission could possibly make banks just as inwardly focused as outwardly focused. Increased compliance and the associated costs this brings will be a challenge banks in many markets have to grapple with.

Interestingly, many of the large technology companies and social payment operators entering the market are not bound by such stringent

regulation as commercial banks and often seek to partner with banks to let them take care of compliance and regulation while they focus on customer experience and innovation.

China's growth

As the world's largest manufacturing economy and exporter of goods and also the world's fastest growing consumer market and second largest importer of goods, China has been growing at significant rates in recent years, and is by far the most important contributor to global growth.

Since initiating market reforms in 1978, GDP growth has averaged nearly 10% a year – the fastest sustained expansion by any economy in history, lifting more than 800 million people out of poverty. Recently China's economy reached US$23.12 trillion in gross domestic product (the total value of goods produced and services provided in one country in a year).

As the Chinese economy continues to rebalance from investment and manufacturing to consumption and services, bankers and officials around the world will be monitoring China for a soft or hard landing from 30 years of explosive growth.

Consolidation in financial services

It is inevitable that consolidation will take place in financial services. In the US alone there are some 5,600 banks, and the global banking markets are ripe for mergers and acquisitions.

With President Trump easing off banking regulations imposed by Barack Obama after the Global Financial Crisis that limited consolidation, there is a high chance consolidation will progress at pace over

the next few years. An early sign of this is the Fifth Third Bancorp US$4.7 billion bid for Chicago's MB Financial, announced in July 2018.

UK small and mid-sized banks are also preparing for a wave of consolidation and takeovers following FirstRand's GBP1.1 billion takeover of Aldermore, and Marlin Bidco's (a jointly owned private equity firm comprising Pollen Street Capital and BC Partners LLP) GBP850 million takeover of Shawbrook Bank.

Clydesdale & Yorkshire Bank CYBG announced a GBP1.7 billion takeover of challenger bank Virgin Money in June 2018.

The Indian Government is also looking to further consolidate its sprawling banking industry following the coming together of Bharatiya Mahila Bank and SBI.

In Germany there is also significant potential for consolidation, with Deutsche Bank sounding out shareholders regarding a potential tilt for large rival CommerzBank.

Further consolidation in the sector is likely to have additional impact on job losses already taking place due to digital transformation and cost-cutting agendas.

Loan losses

Loan loss provisions are an expense set aside as an allowance for uncollected loans and loan payments by banks and financial service companies. This provision is used to cover a number of factors associated with potential loan losses, including bad loans, customer defaults and renegotiated terms of a loan that incur lower than previously estimated payments. To mitigate credit risk, banks will set aside a specific amount as a cushion to absorb expected losses on a bank's loan portfolio, essentially a provision for bad debts.

The subprime issue, global recession, subsequent housing price collapse and increased unemployment caused many banks, particularly in the US, to write off billions of dollars in assets.

Loan loss provisions increased significantly during the recession but have subsided in recent years. As the global economy has recently strengthened, banks' allowances for loan losses as a share of total loans has reduced. However, with significant house price appreciation and record high debt-to-earnings levels in many markets such as Canada, Australia, UK and China, carefully monitoring loan portfolios will be critical moving towards 2020 and beyond.

Interest rates and mortgage costs are starting to rise from historically low levels, and banks will need to keep a very keen eye on loan portfolio management and consumer delinquency rates over the next few years.

Westpac indicated in its recent annual report that properties in possession increased by 175 to 437, mainly as a result of delinquency increases in Western Australia and Queensland. Is this an early sign of increased delinquencies moving forward?

The global housing price increases of the last 10 years, causing associated accelerated consumer debt levels, are likely to be of critical importance to banks over the next few years as they carefully monitor potential loan losses.

Increased technology costs

'The idea of every company having its own technology stack, own banking applications and legacy systems is such a museum of information,' was how one fintech investor and insurance executive described technology in banking at a recent conference I attended.

According to Gartner's technology research the global banking industry will spend approximately US$600 billion on information technology in 2019. The reality is many banks around the world still operate on core systems developed in the 1970s and 1980s. Some of the figures to support these legacy systems are astounding:

- Goldman Sachs has 9,000 software engineers out of a total staff of 34,000.

- Analysts at Citi estimated recently that maintaining legacy systems, investing in new ones and paying IT staff salaries amounts to 15% to 25% of a bank's full annual expense budget.

- Many IT research companies estimate that between 60% and 70% of IT costs are spent on maintaining legacy systems.

Technology core upgrades are however an expensive business, as shown by Commonwealth Bank of Australia's recent replacement of core IT systems by SAP. The original two-year A$580 million project expanded to A$1.3 billion over five years.

As banks across the world – all with their own digital agendas – look to move away from myriad legacy systems that are difficult and costly to manage, significant new capital will be invested in upgrades and enhancements, with a typical upgrade of core banking software taking anywhere between two and five years. Gartner expects IT expenditure in India alone to increase by over 11% to over US$9 billion dollars.

Many banks need to take the bitter pill now and commence core infrastructure upgrades and migration of in-house databases and storage to the cloud. Ultimately investing in new technology can deliver better customer service, improved process efficiencies, and impact internal and external stakeholders positively. That being said, a key challenge in the 2020s will be to change the mindset in many banks from one of a finance company to one of a technology company.

Cost structures

With escalating information technology costs associated with supporting and upgrading core systems coupled with increased investments in cyber-security, banks will need to carefully manage other key input costs to their businesses moving forward. With subdued industry growth in many developed markets and increasing fintech competition, banks are likely to resort to the cost lever to maintain profitability.

I have already touched on some of the changes happening to employment and wage costs. Other direct and indirect costs will come under the microscope too. Professional service fees, technology costs, telecommunications and marketing are all major costs for financial services enterprises, as are travel-related expenses. In an increasingly competitive global banking market, cost efficiencies and leveraging purchasing scale will become very important.

Bancolombia is one company that has been tackling their costs in prudent ways; encouragingly they have also been doing it in a socially and environmentally friendly manner. Let's see what they have been doing.

Travel costs

A self-management tool was implemented for the purchase of air tickets combined with airline negotiations, purchase of promotional airfares and travel policy enhancements, achieving annual savings of US$3.2 million.

Efficiencies for sharing vehicles from and towards the airport amounted to another US$162,000 in savings, and importantly delivered environmental benefits.

Paper and materials savings

By implementing decreased paper forms, better management of printing within the business and utilization of improved scanning technologies, Bancolombia have been able to save US$71,000 and importantly recycle some 15,000 kilograms of paper.

Water and energy efficiency

Water savings, energy-efficiency projects at branches and general recycling have also yielded numerous financial and economic benefits, including:

- air conditioner optimization, saving over 250,000 kWh of electricity per annum
- paper, carton, glass and plastic recycling, amounting to over 300 tonnes generated, with further benefits of US$33 million in income.

Many banks looking to achieve cost savings can learn from how Bancolombia have embraced carefully managing costs with protecting our precious natural environment.

Public perception

Following the well-publicized bank bailouts following the Global Financial Crisis, where taxpayer-funded support provided capital for certain banks under financial distress to restore confidence and stability in the sector, the public has never been so interested in the banking industry.

Bailouts and government assistance have been far reaching, with the UK Government nationalizing Lloyds Bank and Royal Bank of Scotland. The US Government introduced a Financial Stability Plan to support

the financial system. Businesses such as Fannie Mae and Freddie Mac became government sponsored, while others such as AIG, Bank of America and Citigroup received federal aid totaling over US$150 billion. Commerzbank of Germany received over 10 billion in euros in early 2009 following significant losses.

In many other markets, shotgun takeovers and mergers happened during the financial crisis to protect consumers, particularly with some smaller banks.

These taxpayer-funded life support mechanisms are still remembered by many global consumers and businesses, causing the public perception of banking in markets such as the UK, Europe and North America to be somewhat tainted. Perception is improving but customers have long memories.

Throw in recent media reports of bank executives at previously bailed-out banks receiving remuneration packages of above US$10 million and you can see how public perception needs to be very carefully monitored with consumers who are battling low wages growth and higher costs of living.

The recent Banking Royal Commission in my home market of Australia has further shone a spotlight on the sector as it reviews if any of Australia's financial services entities have engaged in misconduct. The initial findings have done little to restore trust with the public, but the positive outcome of the review looks to be a more disciplined and considerate industry going forward.

Banks that are really genuine and customer focused stand to gain the most by winning over a public somewhat disenchanted with the industry. This applies at a time where new market entrants such as platform providers offer a perceived fresh approach and technology companies including Google, Apple and Amazon are generally very well regarded by key customer segments.

Quantitative easing

Quantitative easing is essentially the introduction of new money into the money supply by a central bank. It is designed to stimulate the economy when interest rates are already low. More money is created digitally to make large purchases of assets from the private sector, including pension funds, banks and bonds. The purchases are of such a scale that they push up asset prices, which encourages further selling and investment in other areas to stimulate the economy.

With quantitative easing done on a scale never seen before in many markets such as the UK, China, Europe and the US, central banks globally will need to carefully manage interest rate increases and the gradual unwinding of quantitative easing.

Only as the global economy starts to unwind from this process will we know the real effects on asset prices and global confidence. The next few years will certainly provide the answer to how the strengthened global banking ecosystem can cope with the unwinding of quantitative easing. Bankers and their boards will be monitoring things closely.

Scaling back

Following the excesses of high loan growth and rapid geographical expansion before and just after the Global Financial Crisis, many banks are grappling with the challenge of scaling back operations in non-core markets. For example:

- Since the Global Financial Crisis, Barclays from the UK alone has halved its balance sheet by GBP1 trillion, sold its African business and exited operations in more than a dozen countries.
- ANZ Bank of Australia has sold retail and wealth businesses in Asia, including in Singapore, Hong Kong, China, Taiwan and Indonesia.

- Deutsche Bank has signaled a sharp scale back of its US presence.
- Société Générale have exited non-synergetic markets such as Albania.

Further scaling back is likely as banks renew focus on their core competencies and chosen geographical markets.

Brexit

The uncertainty surrounding the UK's exit from the European Union is providing challenges for that market, with potential knock-on impacts to the wider financial services landscape.

Many banks are spending a tremendous amount of effort adapting to Brexit-related changes. Due to new UK legislation, Barclays have set up a new ring-fenced bank from scratch and migrated some 24 million customers. JP Morgan are moving 300 to 400 jobs around Europe in the short term and modifying some of their legal entities to be able to conduct business the day after Brexit.

An important part of developments will be how UK 'passporting' rights, that allow UK financial companies to sell their services across the EU, will play out. Pre Brexit, a UK bank based in London can sell services within the EU just as easily as domestically.

Also, foreign banks based in the UK – for example, American banks based out of London – can also sell services right across the EU. The UK's Financial Conduct Authority has indicated approximately 5,500 financial companies in the UK currently have EU passporting rights.

As Brexit negotiations progress, many banks with a presence in the UK will be carefully monitoring developments to ensure they can still service the huge EU market with over 500 million people that these passporting capabilities connect them to.

Climate change

The most important challenge facing not only banking but everyone in our world is climate change. I mentioned in chapter one how global temperatures are trending significantly higher, and to support global expansion by 2030 we will require 50% more energy, 40% more water and 35% more food.

Now I'm no scientist, but what I do know is the seasons and weather cycles are dramatically later, hotter and more ferocious on all fronts than when I grew up. Pictured below is the golf course near my parents' house in the UK after a period of high temperatures and hardly any rainfall. This is something that we would not have been seen in prior years.

Overstone Park Golf Course, Northampton, UK July 2018

We have also seen recently in Australia how farmers have been hit terribly by a lack of rainfall, affecting agricultural crops and livestock.

Climate change has the ability to severely impact the global economy through extended droughts affecting agricultural supply, higher rainfall and storms, leading to flooding and affecting food and physical product supply chains. And rising sea levels, hurricanes and more fires bring threats to billions of dollars worth of property that banks lend against.

Climate change presents challenges to the financial sector broadly, including management of physical locations, potential lending losses and write offs, and likelihood of increased insurance claims and premiums.

We must all do everything we can each day to help protect our precious natural environment.

* * *

As you can see, there are many real and emerging challenges ahead for you and the industry. Issues regarding job security, cyber-crime, intense competition, high debt levels and climate change are some of the factors that are playing out around the world as you read this book.

I have purposefully laid all these challenges out because to be successful in financial services or if you are selling to the sector you need to be acutely aware of this environment.

The industry also offers great growth opportunities and an exciting future for people and businesses willing to adapt and transform, as we cover in the exciting chapters ahead.

3. How do you grow and transform in this changing environment?

In this third chapter I'm going to share ideas on how you can grow your bank or financial services business. Whether you're a CEO planning the future path, a VP running a large sales division, a manager accountable for delivering your sales budgets or a new starter working out how to win deals, I aim to share with you here some ideas on how to generate growth for you and your organization.

As we have discussed in prior chapters we are living in the innovation age where customer expectations and demands are shifting higher and faster than ever before. Being customer obsessed, not just *saying* you are customer obsessed, will be more important than ever before. Banks and financial service providers must change their products and sales processes to be much more customer-centric, as this will be of critical importance for growth and indeed survival.

The customer is now making the rules

If financial institutions stand still and rely on what's worked in the past they are on a sure-fire route to becoming an unintended utility, reduced market share and less relevance. Disruption is the new normal, and

today the customer is making the rules. Customer focus will become of crucial importance in this innovation age where clients must be at the center of everything you do.

Customer focus in financial services means that your staff and business are always focused on clients' wants and needs, particularly in a world where these needs are moving rapidly. It requires a shift from credit focus to customer focus, internal to external focus, slow and steady to fast and nimble, because customers can easily get your service elsewhere.

Doing the simple things right and getting the basics working brilliantly while delivering added and personalized value on top to create client delight will be the required recipe, as well as having sales and service teams that are genuinely focused on positive customer outcomes and their success.

Growth opportunities

Growth opportunities are coming forward across the world, whether it be new, smarter ways of doing things in developed markets or reaching previously unbanked sectors in rural communities in developing countries.

A rising middle class across Asia and South America is offering opportunity for banks and new entrants, and 1.5 billion Africans will be of working age by 2050. Will they be the next emerging-market middle class?

Having new growth markets in emerging Africa, Asia, Latin and South America offers market participants great opportunity to not only diversify revenue streams but add new customers. Providing services to these emerging markets will allow banks to grow, particularly if they are from developed markets such as the US and Europe where industry revenues have recently been relatively flat.

Following the geographical scale back after the financial crisis, banks are now back exploring offshore to find fresh opportunities. For example, Citibank is placing a tremendous focus on an emerging Mexico to complement a strong growth focus on the US cards business. HSBC is targeting demographic growth segments, particularly in emerging Asia.

Emerging economies such as Indonesia, Philippines and India are expected to experience strong growth over the next five years, and will be welcome injections to industry profits for market participants operating in these geographies. There is no doubt market competition will intensify in the coming years as incumbents, fintech entrants and established payment networks collide.

With high levels of industry competition and similar levels of product functionalities across providers, all with their own digital strategies, the requirement to have a defined and customer-focused strategy and clear sales proposition will be key. Banks need to become much more efficient at selling multiple value-added customer-centric products to expand revenues and increase returns.

In chapter two I wrote about how having a human-centered, empathetic and creative sales process that cannot be easily automated will benefit individuals and businesses. In the pages that follow I walk you through my TRANSFORM sales process I used to target markets, win clients and grow sales in my 25-year career in institutional financial services.

Much of this methodology was developed and used across high-end institutional sales, but the principles can just as readily be deployed and used across information technology, partnerships and services as these negotiations become more important moving forward. With the challenges ahead for the industry as we approach 2020 and beyond, you must have a good sales process to help you stay ahead of the competition.

Let's start by defining your target market and ideal customer.

Target client and market

In one of my first financial services sales roles I was tasked with selling premium commercial cards in Derbyshire and Nottinghamshire in the North Midlands, UK. This is largely a cost-conscious, working-class area where premium cards were not really accepted or used. *I did not have one sale after six months.* I figured out I needed to be targeting information technology businesses with frequent international travelers, so I asked for a transfer to cover the Heathrow airport business travel area.

I had my first sale within three days.

The key message here is to plan extremely carefully who you are actually targeting. Be clear on where, who and why you want to target them. Start by asking yourself these three questions:

1. What problem does my product or service solve?

2. Why is it remarkable or different?

3. What is the compelling event for customer adoption?

Whether you are a new digital bank looking to attract customers from the growing millennial population, a corporate credit card sales manager looking for small business clients who travel regularly, or an institutional business development manager planning which large clients to target, having a clear strategy and approach to identifying and targeting ideal clients is critically important.

Most salespeople and sales leaders I have met over the years are horrified the day they get given their annual or quarterly target. *How on earth am I going to sign up $2M in new business this year? Where will we get it from? How can we generate $50M of billed revenues this quarter?*

Often the sales team, following distribution of annual sales targets, visit the local pub for a moan and groan about management's unrealistic expectations.

From there, the general observation I have noticed over the years is salespeople, bankers and sales leaders dust themselves off and 'get busy' hoping sales opportunity flows their way, through activity and with an element of praying that opportunity and the 'gimme' (drop in your lap large deal) comes in. But this is reactive and not the best approach – today's financial services managers and executives need to have a methodical approach based on data to plan where the growth is coming from.

Macro- and micro-level planning are important to define your ideal target client characteristics and events that are likely to generate a demand for your service. The below Target Client Analyzer is a great way to help you plan first and foremost where you and your teams should be targeting for sales success.

Make sure you are spending your efforts and time pursuing customers you want based on ideal characteristics and events that generate a demand for your services.

Go ahead and write down what makes the characteristics of your ideal customer and what events can create a demand for your service or product. Also spend some time thinking about what problem your service solves and why it is remarkable.

Then list the characteristics of your least preferred customer and events that are likely to stop a demand for your service; for example, takeover, staffing freeze or technology changes. Determining what your detailed ideal target customer characteristics are will set you apart from many other financial services sales organizations and salespeople, many of which simply pursue the business they don't have as a blanket strategy without validating first if the segment is profitable or the clients a good strategic fit.

Characteristics of ideal customer?	What events can create a demand for our services?
• High cash balances • Over $500M in revenue • International business import or export • Decision maker in Australia • Based within 100 km radius of Sydney CBD • Looking for IT and process efficiencies • Regular international travel	• ERP technology upgrade • Refinancing of business • Merger of companies • Poor service from incumbent • Technical outages at incumbent • Senior staff changes • Infrastructure project • Employee expense requirement
Characteristics of not ideal customer?	**What scenarios stop a demand for our service?**
• Cash swept out of country • Industry in secular decline • Intensive manual support required • Price primary focus as partnership not sought • <$50M in revenues	• Takeover from offshore • Committed to financing elsewhere • Senior staff changes • No corporate card policy

Example ideal client matrix

You will have taken time to strategically plan not only who your ideal target customers are but what their specific profile characteristics are that make them ideal for you to pursue.

Once you have determined your ideal target customer profile you will be able to use industry reports, data analysis and data analytics to build your starting pipeline or target customer list.

As you can see, defining who and where your ideal target customers are is a critical first step in the sales growth process. Determining what problem you are solving for them is of paramount importance, as is understanding what events may generate a demand or reduce demand for your service.

Once you have defined your target market, geography and ideal target clients, the next step is to research them.

Research

You cannot sell to an industry if you don't understand it.

In high-end corporate financial services and banking sales, you simply cannot go and meet someone in an industry if you know nothing about it. Well, you can – but expect a short and average meeting.

Whether it is oil and gas, technology, real estate or another industry, familiarize yourself with the key industry trends and the industry financial supply chain before you meet or target a client. You will be amazed at the difference it actually makes when you do meet the client and how it assists in building industry-based value propositions.

Here's some things for you to think about:

- Do you know the industry headwinds and tailwinds?
- Have you read the client's annual report?
- Have you mapped the business's financial supply chain?
- Do you know who the key people are?
- Can you simply explain their key revenue streams, divisions and major costs?
- Do you know their vision and strategy?
- Do you know the major trends affecting the industry?

> RESEARCH

COST industry analyzer sales planning tool

> Costs

What are the key costs your target client has in running their business?

> Operating environment

Is it a growth industry? What parts of the industry are growing or declining? How much is the industry growing? What changes are affecting the operating environment?

> Sales

What is the sales breakdown for your target client by product and geography? What are the biggest divisions or product revenue streams? Where is the income actually coming from?

> Trends

What key trends are shaping this industry? How is the industry changing? How are industry participants adapting? What are the opportunities and threats for this industry?

Approach

I went to a meeting once with a major international automobile man-ufacturer. I took along six slides all about the automobile industry, the key trends, the customer's financial supply chain metrics and the dis-ruptive trends threatening the industry. There was not one slide about what my business offered. The meeting went for over two hours. And yes, I won the contract.

The message here is customers don't really care about *your* business. They care about *their* business and their problems.

Poor preparation = poor results

The first meeting with a customer can be tough. How do you best approach the meeting to ensure the client gets value and you get the information you require?

Most salespeople know they should do preparation before a client meeting, but many don't have a structure to follow so end up 'winging it' (improvising and proceeding without proper preparation or time to rehearse). After 30 years of strategic sales, I'm still stunned how many salespeople at big organizations poorly prepare for client meetings and think through what they are going to say only in the taxi on the way to the meeting. Well, it's just not good enough in today's business environment.

If you have a proven process to follow it will make it easier to gather all the information you need before the meeting and enable you to have a more strategic conversation during the meeting. Take time to research the customer and their industry in detail.

Changing your approach from 'product sales focused' to 'industry insights focused' will help you progress ideal target clients faster.

The next step in the TRANSFORM sales process is where the rubber really hits the road; it's the first customer discussion, meeting and approach.

The GROWTH Meeting Planner

A pre-meeting client planning tool such as the one following is a great way to help you more efficiently approach the client. It forces you to prepare well, and ultimately facilitates much more strategic and progressive client conversations when you are in the meeting. It also ensures time spent with the client generates value for both parties.

I'm going to break this meeting planner down for you into the key components needed to execute a successful approach and first sales meeting.

> GROWTH

Six minute sales accelerator meeting planner

> Greet

With a smile and friendly, professional demeanor connect with your customer.

> Research

In advance who are you meeting, what is their position and level of influence?
What are the client's macro industry challenges?

> Open

Meeting with clear message regarding what you want to cover off, over what time.
More importantly explain what will be the benefits of spending time with you for the
prospective client.

> What

Key questions do you want to ask, in what order? What questions have you researched and
prepared in advance? Why are they beneficial to the customer?

> Takeaway

What are the two or three points you really want the customer to take away from this
meeting? What are the action points (for both parties)?

> Home

When back at your home or office follow up on your action points promptly and efficiently.

Greet

The first 60 seconds of a customer meeting are critical to establish the tone of the discussion, including your ability to bond with the other person. Be professional and look professional. Be sure to smile, make eye contact, adapt to the other person's body gestures and importantly connect and build rapport. Use small talk to get the conversation flowing about an easy-to-discuss topic such as sports, family, their industry, company-specific news or a common interest.

Research

As previously mentioned, spend time in advance of the customer meeting understanding their industry. Read their website and their annual report. Briefly map their core business model including major revenue streams, and complete the COST template from the previous step. Research the company's strategy and focus areas. Research the key people in the business and research the people you are meeting. (Is there any common thread? Have you worked at the same company before, studied at the same university, or do you follow the same industry associations?)

Open

Being clear what you want to cover off in the meeting is important, as is clarification of time available. Make sure you explain the benefits to the customer of spending time with you early on in the meeting. Find a hook to interest them. For example:

Cathryn, I just wanted to double check we still have 30 minutes today to discuss some key trends in your industry and some ideas to make savings in your financial supply chain – is that okay with you?

What

Prepare what you want to discuss before the meeting. I recommend preparing a good range of open-ended questions to help you understand the customer needs and also help the customer to discover their needs. Remember, open-ended questions require a lengthier response and usually start with words or phrases such as 'explain', 'describe', 'please tell me', 'which' or 'how'. Also, consider preparing some higher impact questions that get the customer to evaluate or reflect.

Examples of pre-prepared high-impact questions are:

I noticed a, b and c is happening in your sector. What are the impacts of this on your business?

How do you feel about the required implementation of x, y and z in your industry?

Takeaway

Be clear on the two or three key points you want the customer to take away from meeting you. Really think this through well before the client meeting. Repeat the points in the meeting if you have to, as long as the customer is clear on what your key messages are. You have worked hard to get the meeting and possibly spent some time traveling to the customer site – don't lose the chance to leave your two or three key takeaway messages.

Home

Follow up promptly (same day, before going home), summarizing the conversation and asking for confirmation you have correctly understood the discussion, opinions, issues and agreed next steps.

Be sure to follow up on your actions quickly and efficiently. It demonstrates you can execute, and builds confidence with the prospective customer.

* * *

As we can see there are many elements to a successful first meeting, from the initial connection over the first 60 seconds to the way you present yourself and the pre-preparation work you have completed. So, prepare well for your next meeting by completing a pre-meeting planner.

However, no part of the sales process is more important than the next stage: clearly understanding the customer's needs.

Needs analysis

I once lost a competitive pitch to a major industrial company. After our competitor was announced as the winner, I reached out to the competitor salesperson, who I knew. He'd had four times the meetings with the client than me before submitting their winning proposal.

My competition understood the target client way better than me. My six months of work on the RFP (request for proposal) were lost, however I'd made one of my biggest ever sales learnings: you're toast if you don't understand your customers' needs better than your competition.

Developing a deep understanding of your clients

The needs analysis is arguably the most important step in the sales process, and it should never be overlooked or rushed through. Good solutions ultimately begin with a deep understanding of client needs.

If you're selling something complex in financial services such as integrated transaction banking or expense management solutions, the needs analysis is likely to take several hours and often multiple meetings across various stakeholders.

To be a highly effective salesperson who is configuring solutions around client needs, you have to first understand what those needs are. So often I see salespeople trying to sell too early before they have understood the underlying client needs. You have to earn the right to advance to the next stage of the process.

Imagine going to your doctor and you're not feeling well, with pains all over your body.

> *Patient:* 'I'm not feeling well at all – I'm really not good.'
>
> *Doctor:* 'Take these tablets three times a day and come in for an operation Tuesday next week and you will be okay.'

How would you feel? The doctor has diagnosed a solution without understanding your needs.

How do you feel when you are approached in a shopping center, airport or store to sell you something immediately without understanding your needs? Basically, the salesperson hasn't earned the credibility or right to advance to sell you anything.

I went to a store a few weeks ago to buy a new vacuum cleaner and the sales agent in the store was employed by one of the manufacturers on a commission basis, not employed by the store. All this person was concerned about was selling the brand they worked for to earn revenue; they didn't care if one of the many other vacuum cleaners better met my needs. In fact, they did not even understand my needs. It was a horrible sales experience from a customer perspective because they were only focused on themselves and their outcome, not mine.

Please spend time being more like a doctor (not the above doctor) when you consult with your clients.

Why is this potential client buying?

No one buys until they realize there is a level of dissatisfaction with the current situation. People move forward with change when the value (increased revenues, reduced costs, reduced risks, increased efficiency) of the new situation is clearly better than the current status.

Have a strategic discussion with each potential client about their industry and challenges. Use an industry analyzer mapping tool (see earlier in this chapter) to provoke open discussion and focus conversation on the customer's business and industry environment.

Read an industry report before meeting the client to gain an appreciation of the current industry growth in the client's market and globally. Here's some issues to consider:

- Is the client in an industry experiencing secular growth trends or are they in an industry with flat or declining revenues such as print and newspapers, where cost savings will be high on the agenda?

- What are competitors doing in their industry?

- What new products or developments are changing their industry?

- What systems, technology, products and processes are your client's competitors using?

- How does your target client currently compare to industry or market best practice?

Start discussions at a high, strategic, macro-business level and work to more micro-level product discussions. Don't rush to be talking about your products or services too early – there is a danger you will try to sell too early.

Keep questioning and dialogue light and natural, and don't make it seem like an interrogation or interview.

To help you with this process I've developed the MICE approach. An example MICE four-level client needs assessment questioning funnel for the banking industry is shown here.

Macro discussion

Business environment
Industry situation

Industry insights

Key industry shifts
Industry metrics and forecasts
New technologies

Client discussion

Customer financial supply chain
Major costs major revenues
Receivables/payables/liquidity

Expected discussion

Transaction banking
Expense management
Merchant processing
International trade

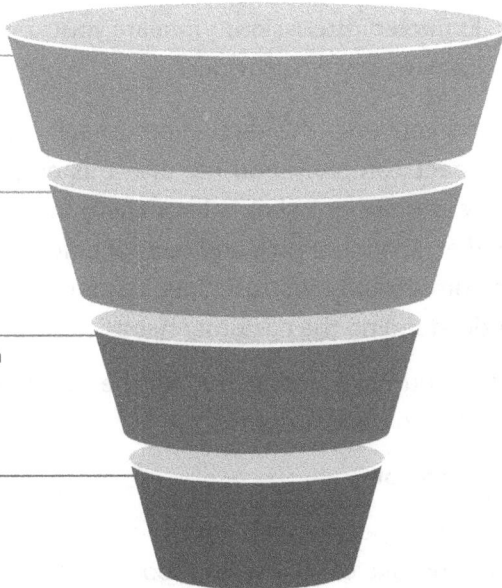

Some questions you can ask

Here are some examples of high-level questions you can ask during the needs analysis phase. These of course need to be adapted to the relevant industry and client:

- **Macro discussion:** 'I understand you trade significantly in US dollars. What are the impacts of the US dollar strengthening to your business?'

- **Industry discussion:** 'I read tariffs are being amended for your industry. What are the impacts to your financial supply chain and end customers?'

- **Client discussion:** 'How do you currently manage corporate travel, meals and entertainment?', 'What are the major business challenges in your import division currently?'

- **Expected discussion:** 'What are your key needs from a transaction banking system provider?'

When you're in the discussion, imagine you worked for the client prospect company. You can use this as an opportunity to educate the customer on what is happening in their industry and the wider market. Share the pros and cons of different points of view and topics you discuss to build trust. Spend as much time as you need to on truly understanding the customer needs.

Once you have understood all the customer needs the next step is issuing a proposal, right?

Well, it's not.

Many salespeople make this mistake; in fact, it is the most common sales mistake of all – selling too early. You should take one extra step that will help your conversion rates soar. That step is summarizing the situation. It probably took me 20 years to properly learn this sales technique, as I was always taught in all the training courses I attended that I should deeply understand the clients needs then issue a proposal.

By introducing the extra step of summarizing the current state scenario versus ideal state requirements before issuing proposals, your sales conversion rates will significantly increase.

Summarizing the situation

The importance of really listening to your potential customers

Demonstrating you are really listening to the customer, understanding their needs and summarizing their ideal state vision is critical in the sales process.

Some years ago, I met a boutique infrastructure investment business working in Australia. To be honest, I didn't expect much from the meeting, but I researched the client, listened to their needs and summarized exactly what they were looking for. Essentially the client wanted a clear and simple plan to manage 12 payments on a time-critical deadline. After summarizing what they required, their ideal state vision and how we could execute urgent payments to help them realize this vision, we were appointed within two days to handle a multi-billion-dollar take-over settlement.

'Summarize' – according to the *Cambridge Dictionary* – means:

> To express the most important facts or ideas about something or someone in a clear and short form.

The step of summarizing the current situation is one many salespeople overlook as they eagerly move to the pitch or proposal stage after the needs analysis.

By taking this one additional step, to summarize your understanding of client requirements and their vision of the ideal state, you demonstrate you have been listening, you confirm what the real client issues are, and you speed up the sales process. This additional sales step also allows you to qualify out opportunities that are *not* ready to move to the stage of being finalized with a proposal, and ultimately means you introduce a higher win rate to your proposals submitted.

Here is an example of how summarizing current situation and ideal state works:

Current situation	Ideal state
Poor visibility of company cash as multiple banking systems used.	One treasury reporting dashboard to monitor group cash balances through one portal.
Wasted time as different systems used in different geographic locations.	One common system used across all locations with one common log in.
No visibility on employee expenses as electronic expenditure data not received.	Daily electronic data feed providing itemized line-by-line employee expense visibility and accountability.

By confirming with the client what the current situation and issues are and your understanding of what the client ideal state looks like, you build a picture of what you need to finalize in your final pitch or proposal as the solution. You have sold nothing at this point, just determined the current state and ideal state.

Get everything on the table

At this stage of the sales process, ask the client if there is anything else. Ask if there are any other issues or problems you have not discussed. Ensure you get all issues and challenges on the table from the client before you propose anything.

Ask the client if they are open to working with you to address the challenges presented with a goal of delivering the ideal solution.

At this point they will say *yes* or *no*.

If they say *yes*, you can close the transaction there and then, or if that's not appropriate, you can move to the next step, which is finalizing a tailored and customized pitch or proposal.

If they say *no*, ask why. It could be there is a competing project in the business that means they have no time to look at this project now; it could be that all issues have not been clarified to the customer's satisfaction; it could be the customer has further requirements for their ideal state that have not been defined.

In some ways it's good if they say *no* at this stage, because you are not put in a scenario where you do all the work of a detailed proposal when they are not ready to proceed. It also means the customer is communicating with honesty to you.

Spend as much time on this part of the sales process as needed until the customer says *yes, I'm ready to proceed to address these issues*. Bear in mind that even if your solution is perfect, the time and priority for their business also has to be right.

Earning the right to advance the process

You need to earn the right to advance to the next stage of the sales process when the time is right for the client. By spending time here, more transactions will positively close right here or go to the next stage of the sales process (finalizing a proposal). Transactions will have a much higher conversion rate because you will be sending proposals to people who have said *yes* to delivering their ideal state vision.

This stage of the sales process – summarizing the situation – is critical as it puts on the line what issues need to be addressed. You need to make the customer see through their eyes the pain points and realize for themselves it's time to act to reach the ideal state.

Do not move to the next stage of submitting the proposal until the customer has said they are ready to proceed there.

When the client is ready, move to the next stage of finalizing a tailored pitch or proposal based on the clients' ideal state requirements and watch your win rates soar.

Finalize

Once your potential client has given you permission to move on to the next stage, make the proposal or presentation you provide to finalize the win all about the customer's challenges, concerns and issues. Explain step by step how you will implement your solution to address the client's challenges and deliver their ideal state vision.

I have seen and attended thousands of presentations over the years – good, bad and ugly. I'm going to share with you here what I've learned from this.

Submitting your final proposal

When you are submitting your final proposal or presentation, I recommend three key things:

- Centre the proposal on customer issues and their ideal state vision.

- Make it 90% about the customer's business and 10% about your business.

- Keep the presentation or proposal below 10 slides or pages, and explain simply how you implement.

Start the presentation with a hook that grabs the customer's attention, and make the proposal really focused on them. Customers don't really

care about all the awards you have won, the historical steps in your 200-year business evolution, or your wonderful multi-level management team.

They care about *their* business and reducing costs, increasing revenues and reducing risks. At the same time the people you're presenting to want recognition, good reward, no project mess-ups, and to look good for the work they are doing on this project-buying decision with you.

Involve your audience in the presentation to make it interactive and ask questions at crucial moments. You will make your audience feel involved, keep them interested, and importantly allow them to explore outcomes through their own answers.

Also, don't be afraid to use appropriate humor during your presentation, use stories if you can, and give examples showing how you will benefit the client. Don't simply read from your slides.

Use visuals to summarize key points. For example, if you are going to save the customer 25%, it's much more powerful in a graphic.

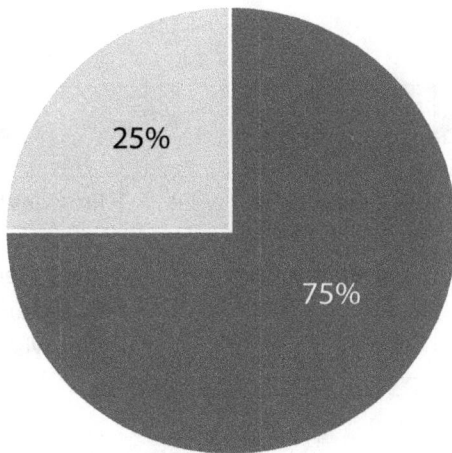

Preparing and rehearsing your presentation

I recommend rehearsing for all major pitches or proposal presentations at least four times, particularly if you are a large business with multiple people in attendance. The rehearsal and practice is so important today when competition is so high and many suppliers may offer a similar product or service.

I promise you, the first rehearsal will be terrible, the second rehearsal will be average, the third rehearsal will be okay and the fourth rehearsal will be good. By the fifth pitch (your one to the client) everything will be well coordinated and you will deliver a high-quality presentation.

Steve Jobs used to spend two days practicing his pitch before a major product launch. The outcome was a very impactful presentation talked about around the world.

Ultimately, it's the 1% or 2% differentials throughout the sales process that add up by the end for the winning mandate, so please don't rush this step and make sure you prepare well. Detailed below is a format I use to give crisp, condensed presentations and proposals that are customer centric.

Presentation step	Purpose	Benefit
Introduction and high-level summary/ agenda	To clearly set out what you plan to cover and benefits to client.	Provides initial benefit statement to client and gives client opportunity to add anything else they wish to cover.

Presentation step	Purpose	Benefit
Current state situation summary	To share the analytical work you have done on assessing the customer's current arrangements during the needs analysis.	Gives the customer opportunity to raise objections to be addressed. Acts as additional trigger for customer to see pain of current state challenges.
Ideal state summary	To detail to the customer your understanding of what their ideal state vision looks like.	Allows customer to see how improvements will look in their ideal blue-sky world.
Solution summary	To explain how your tailored solution delivers the ideal state.	Delivers a customized solution to address client challenges and deliver their ideal state vision.
Implementation plan	To practically explain how your service gets implemented.	Demonstrates you have a proven implementation methodology and know how to logically implement to realize benefits for the customer.
Pricing	Brings pricing in at a time when ideal state and implementation benefits have been explained.	Allows pricing to be 'sandwiched' between the benefits of ideal state and benefits summary.

Presentation step	Purpose	Benefit
Summary	To reconfirm the client's issues, what ideal state looks like and how you will deliver.	Explains full value of your solution, including what problems it addresses and the benefits generated.
Next steps	To keep transaction moving forward and not lose momentum.	Provides clear, agreeable follow-up actions everyone has heard and is committed to deliver.
Thank you	To appreciate client for the time they have invested with you.	Shows good manners, humbleness and professionalism.

So, the tailored customer proposal is submitted, complete with a clear explanation of how you will implement to realize the benefits. Now you need to progress and move through the next stage quickly, which is closing the deal and obtaining approval to proceed.

Obtaining a *yes*

Always sandwich the price between benefits, just like a hamburger. At this point you have a deep understanding of the client's current state and vision for their ideal state. They have said to you that they want to work with you to resolve their challenges and concerns.

You have presented how your solution delivers their goals and answered any objections they have. You have also clearly explained how you will implement their ideal state vision.

After summarizing current state/ideal state/delivered benefits state, ask for the business.

'So, you're ready to proceed to realize the benefits?'

Have an in-principle proposal or mandate letter on hand that can be signed off to commence progress. Make it easy to transact and explain clearly how you will implement.

If the customer still has concerns, ask them:

'What issues do you see that are preventing you from proceeding now? Let's discuss them now while I'm here.'

A useful closing technique structure to follow is:

Closing step	**Purpose**	**Benefit**
Summarize current state	Shows customer how current world is not as it should be and needs improvement.	Makes client realize pain of current state and reinforce it's time to act.
Present ideal state	You are summarizing what client has described to you as their ideal solution.	Shows customer what an improved world looks like.
Benefit state	Explains how your solution delivers the ideal state in customer's mind.	Shows clearly what product solution is and how it is implemented.
Ask for business	So you are ready to proceed?	Gets a clear *yes* or *no* confirmation.

Closing step	Purpose	Benefit
Answer any final objections	To resolve any final issues or concerns while you are there. ('What issues do you see that are preventing you from proceeding now? Let's discuss them now while I'm here.')	Reaches a point of agreement.
Sign proposal to proceed letter	Provides high-level summary of what you will deliver.	Obtains a written agreement to proceed.
Implementation	To deliver solution, sign off any product-specific documentation (terms and conditions) and scope-specific user requirements.	Allows you to wrap up any more complex documentation sign off in the implementation process when the project is moving.

If you have followed all the steps methodically up to this process you should be aiming to close 80% of the proposals you submit.

In scenarios where the client still can't decide or wants to revisit in six months, ask them:

> *'For my own learning and development, is there anything I could have done differently to make you feel more comfortable obtaining the benefits from your ideal state solution?'*

It is best to learn and refine from the few transactions that do not positively progress.

* * *

So, we've smoothly moved through the sales process by asking for the business and sandwiching the price between the benefits of current state and the ideal state. We've also clearly explained how we implement at a high level and provided a letter of intent or agreement to get the project moving.

The next step is to deliver the promise and ensure you deliver what you have sold and that the client is delighted.

Realize revenues

The first large credit card transaction deal I ever negotiated and closed involved three-way meetings, advanced financial modeling, and took six months to close. Once we had won the business we made the transaction so simple the customer just had to sign a pre-completed form and enter 'approve' on the payment system for a pre-loaded payment.

The message here is, make your implementation simple and explain how you are going to do it in your proposal or pitch.

Load the first transaction for the customer, fill out the paperwork so they just have to sign it, give them a free trial or set them up with easy-to-use templates. Whatever you do, make it easy to implement and do business with you.

Handover

It never ceases to amaze me how many salespeople win the business and then walk away. Often there is no, or a very poor, handover to the implementation manager, account manager or customer service team.

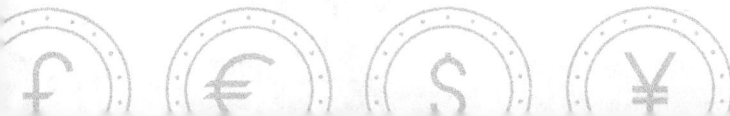

Always be there to ensure your sale gets delivered efficiently and to the customer's satisfaction. The best salespeople genuinely care about the product and service delivery to the client they have been working with for so long.

Be sure to attend implementation kick-off meetings and weekly progress calls, and monitor post-implementation reviews. Trust me, you will learn so much more about your customer and your business's service delivery through this process that the benefits will vastly outweigh the time invested. You will learn product tips to help you sell your service in innovative new ways, you will see real-world examples of what your business really delivers, and you will build trusted business relationships that last a lifetime.

I have listed below some key steps in the implementation process that I recommend you follow to have a happy customer and glowing future client testimonial. My recommendation is, as the sales lead you steadily let the implementation manager and account or service manager take over client responsibility through this process but be involved to oversee things the whole way through.

Implementation step	Purpose	Benefit
Provide all proposal, pricing, and meeting notes and pertinent transaction materials discussed with the client to implementation manager.	Brings implementation manager up to speed on client requirements.	Acts as good basis of information to scope actual requirements.

Implementation step	Purpose	Benefit
Meet implementation manager in person to discuss transaction that has been won, including any key or critical points of delivery for the client.	To further validate implementation manager's understanding of client and solution that has been sold to them.	Provides implementation manager with a clear understanding of client journey so far, including customer pain points and solution deliverables.
Introduce implementation manager to client in face-to-face meeting to discuss high-level implementation methodology. Also use session as high-level scoping of requirements.	To give customer confidence appropriate resources and processes are being allocated to the onboarding of their business.	Acts as a formal kick off for the project, allows implementation manager to build initial relationship, and gets client familiar with delivery process. Facilitates gathering of key implementation scope requirements.
Scope document	Confirms understanding in writing with customer of what will be implemented and who will be involved. Defines roles and responsibilities and high-level timelines.	Makes everything crystal clear from the outset of implementation and acts as a written source to refer back to when monitoring progress.

Implementation step	Purpose	Benefit
Project plan	High-level project plan showing steps and stages in the implementation process.	Clearly defines what needs to be done by whom to deliver a complete and on-time implementation.
Weekly status summary report	To summarize what work has been completed and highlight any known risks.	Great high-level written structure of where project is at and progress made.
Introduce account manager or customer service manager	To bring account manager into client relationship at the appropriate time.	Brings account manager up to speed on solution implementation. Familiarizes client to account manager and starts to seamlessly hand over business from sales to account management.
Weekly project meeting or video conference	To track and monitor implementation and project progress.	Keeps momentum moving so project does not stall. Good for highlighting and resolving potential risks and roadblocks that always come up.

Implementation step	Purpose	Benefit
Onsite go-live support and training	To show support for your customer when they make first transactions or use your system or service for the first time.	Demonstrates you are there to ensure the project is a success. Note: While these meetings can be done by phone or video, I highly recommend being onsite in person with the client the day the rubber hits the road. It shows meaningful commitment to a long-term relationship.
Post-implementation review	To obtain feedback on how well the solution was implemented and ensure it meets customer needs.	Provides feedback on real customer experience and offers ideas to improve future client experiences. Shows you and your business are serious that what was sold gets delivered.
Six- and twelve-month value delivery review	To ensure the client has achieved the benefits from the solution sold.	Provides real feedback and learning regarding what your solution has delivered. Offers great opportunity to gain client testimonial on project success.

You can probably hear how passionate I am about getting the implementation right, delivering on the promise and realizing the revenues. The best financial services salespeople are the ones that truly care and follow through to ensure great customer outcomes.

So, we've taken the client through our whole sales process, from determining the ideal customer through to winning the business and realizing the benefits for their business and our business.

We now have to carefully grow, nurture and manage the business won and be sure to never neglect it.

Management

It's much easier to sell more to an existing customer than to a new customer. For most businesses, 80% to 90% of revenues come from existing customers. These customers are the ones that ultimately cover your business's fixed costs, pay the wages, facilitate payment to suppliers and generate a profit. But all too often this area is neglected in business. Looking after existing customers is just not as 'sexy' as going for new business. My advice is to spend time really looking after your customers, nurture them, build new capabilities with them, and develop trust-based relationships with them. Develop strategic relationship account plans with your customers and use them to help sell more value to existing clients.

Develop strategic relationship account plans with your customers and use them to help sell more value to existing clients

There are four key types of existing clients, as detailed in the diagram following. The goal should be to migrate customers from the bottom left of this quadrant over time to the top right through account planning methodologies that link the client's strategy, mission and vision to your ability to help them achieve their outcomes.

Relationship focus	Partnership focus
Wants a close working relationship Seeks advice and guidance	Values a long-term, win–win, mutually beneficial relationship
Transactional	**Informational**
Heavy focus on price Commoditized approach Holds product knowledge	Wants educating on products and market trends Interested in information about your business

It's so much easier to upsell and grow revenues with a client you already have or expand the relationship to new divisions or entities. Spend at least 50% of your sales and marketing costs looking after your existing business; the investment will be worth it.

Effective account and relationship management can add tremendous value to your business in multiple areas across service, people connectivity, revenue generation and product development. The table opposite gives some useful ideas of how account management done well can be beneficial to your customer's business and your business.

Effective account or relationship management done well offers great business expansion opportunities. It is absolutely critical to look after the business you have worked so hard to win and onboard.

I have witnessed so many times in my career clients that have been neglected once they have been won. The best financial services businesses are also fixated on looking after their existing clients to support both businesses' long-term growth.

Service	People
Ensures any major customer issues are tracked, monitored and resolved in a timely manner. Acts as a gauge of client satisfaction during regular review meetings. Allows you to deliver additional insights such as transactional analysis, peer analysis, benchmark reviews and process optimization.	Facilitates building of further client contacts to deepen and cement the relationship across key personnel and key influencers. Provides the opportunity to introduce your senior staff to senior staff of the client to further strengthen the relationship.
Revenues	**Product**
Offers ability to expand relationship to other products, divisions or markets. Reinforces your value proposition and allows introduction of enhanced products or new services. Offers opportunities for referrals and testimonials to generate extra business. Offers opportunities for cross-selling and upselling.	Confirms the product or service sold is meeting the customer's needs. Potential for customer focus groups to help develop further value-added capabilities. Offers the starting point to develop case studies and thought leadership papers to use in other customer acquisition activities.

Benefits of effective account management matrix

By executing the TRANSFORM end-to-end sales methodology I have shared here, I have no doubt you and your business can penetrate new growth markets, build a stronger sales pipeline and ultimately convert and win more business faster.

With all these new ideas, let's go ahead now and look at the future for financial services and how you can leverage these new skills and new ideas to grow your results and the business you work for, into 2020 and beyond.

4. The future

In this chapter, I'm not going to predict the future, but I am going to share some of the key developments taking place in global financial services and across technology more broadly, to help you build your own perspective on the future of financial services and importantly figure out your plan for succeeding in the industry.

Predicting the future is notoriously difficult, and some would say a fool's game. Often when we look back it is amazing how much changes and how much stays the same. I would never have believed 10 years ago while carrying my first Blackberry business mobile that I would today be trading shares, managing hotel rooms, videoing friends for free, snapping great photos and checking weather conditions all from my smartphone, whenever and wherever I want to.

The massive impact of technology

We live in a world now where technology is permeating every corner of the planet and allowing populations to connect, communicate and conduct commerce more efficiently than ever. In fact, one could argue

that the biggest five customer growth markets now defined by population are:

- Google Android: 2.3 billion
- Facebook: 2.23 billion
- China: 1.41 billion
- India: 1.35 billion
- Apple: 1.3 billion.

In Google's recent annual report they explain how 'many companies get comfortable doing what they have always done, making only incremental changes. This incrementalism leads to irrelevance over time, especially in technology, where change tends to be revolutionary, not evolutionary'. They also explain how 'Google is not a conventional company and they do not intend to become one'.

I think businesses and individuals working in corporate banking and financial services need to learn from this approach. If we get comfortable doing what we have always done we are going to wither and die. We need to find new ways to not be conventional and comfortable, but to bring fresh approaches to reinventing ourselves and our businesses to deliver compelling value propositions for our customers.

Our success as businesses and individuals will be based on our ability to create new value propositions and approaches that add real value to our customers and delight them. We need to transform ourselves because the world and its customers are doing it. In a world that is moving faster than ever before, I encourage you to control what you can control, focus on the customer, have fun and never forget the great opportunities before all of us.

Technology in banking

Technology is having an impact across the whole world. It's opening markets to people who were previously excluded through smartphone access. New, powerful platforms such as Facebook, Airbnb and Uber are transforming industries and consumer experiences.

In banking a multitude of new providers are emerging based on new platform technology, and technological change and digital transformation are being embraced by established banks around the world.

As previously mentioned, over the next few years massive investments are scheduled from the banking industry into digital technology and transformation. The important balance to this will be to center these investments around what the customer requires, rather than mirroring what the competition is doing.

Key analysis in this book has been researched from over 50 annual reports from technology companies, global banks, commercial banks and payment providers in the US, Europe, Middle East, Australia, Africa, Scandinavia, Asia, China, South America and more. After a while, many of these annual reports start to sound and look a bit the same. Every bank wants to have the best mobile banking application and is undergoing digital transformation to provide better customer service, focusing on human-centered design and deploying agile project processes to deliver process efficiencies and improved customer service. In my opinion there is not enough content about helping the customer in these reports. Moving towards 2020, if we don't have the customer as our number one focus we are less likely to have a successful business.

Interestingly, many banks – often in the same country – often have near identical goals and strategies. But how can every bank be the best for customer service and have the best digital proposition? Also,

banks are having to adapt to new entrants from the fintech area that are using technology to provide fast, cheap and secure solutions.

Ultimately, successful banks and financial institutions moving forward will be the ones squarely focused on delighting customers and having a great combination of 100% digital and 100% human offering. In other words, when a customer wants to deal and transact digitally they can do that. When a customer wants human interaction and personal advice they can do that.

Financial services companies need to be driven by how the customer wants to transact. For example, a 25-year-old millennial may never need to visit a branch and be happy sending payments through Facebook Messenger. But, with a rapidly ageing global population, a 65-year-old retiree or part-time worker may want personal assistance in a comfortable private lounge environment to manage investments or physical transactions.

The digital transformation

Digital transformation in banking is ultimately a key response to meeting rising customer expectations set by technologies used in other industries, where speed and scale of competitor offerings and platforms are fast and global. The impact of technology in banking is becoming the number one board issue alongside cyber-security. CEOs are having to balance costly transformation expenses that deliver long-term benefits against putting pressure on existing margins from a relatively stable (now) customer base.

Information technology research company Gartner estimates that banks' spending on technology will increase in 2019 to over US$600 billion, an all-time high. These costs generally must be funded in ways without impacting profits, a very difficult balancing act.

In just one market alone, Canada, competing banks are deploying significant investment:

- Royal Bank of Canada will invest C$3 billion in new technology this year and has made 1,000 digital hires in the last two years.

- Bank of Montreal are increasing expenditure on technology, with an increase of 17% declared in their recent annual report.

- CIBC Canada are planning to invest C$1 billion per annum in new technologies.

These are changes taking place in just one market where most banks are driving a digital agenda and focusing on being the number one digital bank. The story and messages are the same in Australia, UK, Singapore, South American countries, Europe and all around the world.

Many banks have embedded digital into their overarching strategy, reporting into the most senior levels of the company. Royal Bank of Scotland in the UK have created a Technology and Innovation Committee of the Board to oversee and monitor this strategic direction, in what has become one of the most important areas of focus for the bank.

Technology is going to need to be embraced across all businesses in financial services, given more and more of the core competency will be integration and moving data efficiently and securely around. More IT specialists will be joining bank boards and management teams.

But don't forget the human side

Personally, while I think digital transformation is critical for banks to compete, I believe as previously mentioned many businesses will cut staff too deep during this wave of digital transformation. It's important for banks to understand with demographic change that not every customer is a 25-year-old millennial.

I talked earlier on about my better half Jessica being caught up in the quick-fire branch closure approach. Many individuals will still want the human connection in a relaxed environment when buying their first home or making significant financial investment decisions.

I understand that consumers will not need to visit branches to bank checks, perform ID checks or withdraw cash from ATMs as much, but I firmly believe there is a role to play for empathetic personal consultants to help customers achieve their financial aspirations.

The businesses that get the right mix between the PeopleBank and the TechnologyBank will do well. Banks will need to offer security and familiarity to an ageing demographic wanting security and safety and a growing millennial customer base wanting speed and functionality. Ultimately banks will need to provide a strong financial ecosystem with strong partners and great retail financial experiences in key foot-traffic hubs where branches are likely to compete against the new retail experience being delivered by the likes of Apple. (Are you one of the many that are surprised by Apple's significant investment in great physical stores?)

Staffless and paperless branches

One theme rapidly emerging in banking is a reshaped branch experience. Most banks recognize that maintaining face-to-face interaction is important with customers to provide them a feeling of security regarding where their money is, and at the same time offering an avenue to build customer loyalty and provide improved servicing and cross-selling opportunities.

More and more banks are moving away from the 'military-style counters' where the attendant is securely locked in a physical serving booth,

to more open-plan experiences that generate a more pleasant customer experience.

ANZ Bank's flagship branch at Martin Place in the center of Sydney was designed by a specialist design company and based upon detailed analysis of customer flows and journey analysis. Upon entering the store, customers are presented with a range of digital banking options including free wi-fi, smart ATMs and iPads for customer use. There is even a three-storey high 'digital vertical garden' on display to make customers feel relaxed.

Other examples include:

- Commercial Bank of Canada has opened over 100 banking centers across the country based on a more open concept that fosters more relaxed interactions with customers.

- Malaysia's CIMB Bank has teamed up with convenience store retailers in Indonesia to offer responsive mobile bank services.

- Emirates Bank in the Middle East have completely renovated branches to make them more 'high touch, high tech', with paperless banking and support from friendly service ambassadors.

- At Royal Bank of Scotland branches in the UK, TechXperts in branches are helping customers better understand how mobile and online banking services can assist them.

Smarter branches and paperless processes are definitely a trend to watch moving towards 2020, with many banks focusing on processes to streamline business and personal account opening with digital signatures provided on an iPad. Time will tell if branches move in the direction of Amazon's Go store, where you just walk in, grab what you need and walk out. It's probably a little bit difficult to walk into a store and grab a mortgage just after you have done your food shopping … but you never know.

The future workplace

New technologies such as artificial intelligence, robotics, video and machine learning are quickly reshaping the workplace in financial services and more broadly. Researchers at McKinsey & Co estimate a mid-point of 400 million workers being displaced due to automation in their 2017 *Future of Work* publication.

Artificial intelligence and automation are causing tremendous economic transformation opportunities, particularly in banking where many processes are still manual and labor intensive. The financial services workforce of the future will need to understand where these technologies will be more efficient than them, and pivot and adapt to these changes by learning new skills that are not easily automated.

Globally, more people will be changing careers and adopting new roles within the industry to work alongside highly efficient machines and technology. Now is a good time to be upskilling and re-skilling through new self-education and courses.

Video and webinar meetings are set to explode, as is virtual working. Financial services will start to reap the benefits of cloud-based collaboration tools such as Google Hangouts across multiple devices. Devices will be used to assist us with productivity at work and home, including developments such as Google's Home and Amazon's Alexa.

More freelancers and entrepreneurs will enter the industry, whether they be fintechs directly trying to compete or digital marketing consultants and social media managers to optimize social media–related revenues. Freelancers, self-employed staff and entrepreneurs will become an ever-expanding part of the global workforce. In fact, Upwork's recent employment report predicts that by 2027 most of the US workforce will be freelancers.

New technologies are going to dramatically change the way work-places operate, with high-productivity tools facilitating coordination and project management across teams. And with automation driving digital transformation, new jobs are also going to emerge as new opportunities come forward. Machine learning roles, virtual reality skills, app development, search engine optimization, online marketing specialists and video banking consultants are all new emerging roles we have never seen before.

Important skills for the future of work are going to be critical thinking, creativity, people skills, STEM (science, technology, engineering and mathematics) and SMAC (social, mobile, analytics and cloud). The ability to manage and coordinate virtual contract teams will be of increasing importance. We are also likely to see personal productivity managers, given the amount of distractions we all face on a daily basis from social media, emails and digital advertising.

There is even likely to be a burgeoning employment market in space-related travel (although probably not by 2020). Any volunteers for the first financial services sales representative covering the territory of Mars? I'm sure there are some takers as sales managers always want bigger sales territories.

Staff training and upskilling

The changes brought about by technology and the future workplace will require banks to look at their staff training programs in different ways. Upskilling and retraining of staff in financial services will be a key theme over the next decade.

For people to keep up with and work alongside highly efficient machines and digital colleagues, new and different skills will be required. This will be important for many banks, which often have many mid-life workers

who have grown up doing a similar role in one organization; for example, credit managers and branch tellers. These people and many others will need to learn new skills to adapt to new roles, or adapt higher level non-automatable skills for current roles.

Company-sponsored training programs will be critical to prevent job losses and to find new ways to better utilize staff. In reality, machines often cannot automate 100% of a person's role, maybe only 20%, so the question will be, how do we invest and retrain our people to get the best return out of their released time?

Alongside technology investment there will be a renewed focus on company training program investment to meet the more varied needs of a diverse workforce. At the same time, maintaining a strong brand, values and long-term strategy will be required to retain key performers and in-demand digitally skilled employees.

Here's what some of the banks around the world are doing:

- Lloyds Bank in the UK is making their biggest ever investment in people by increasing staff training and development by 50% to 4.4 million hours per annum.

- OCBC of Singapore is continuously reskilling and upskilling more than 29,000 employees through more than 3,200 training and development programs. This is equivalent to 7.9-person days of average training per employee.

- The National Bank of Kuwait has an extensive staff training program where middle management develop the skills required to be better managers. Topics covered include developing and managing people and skills, adaptive leadership, conflict and change management, effective communication skills, and performance management and talent retention.

- Qatar National Bank has tied up with Oxford University and Essex University in the UK to develop new digital banking programs. The bank sees innovation as employee-driven as well as market-driven, meaning they will leverage employees to identify opportunities for innovation daily.

- Royal Bank of Canada is doing similar through encouraging employees to have an 'always learning' mindset and encouraging the setting of ambitious goals.

One of my recommendations to bankers and financial services sales managers across the globe is to upskill on technology. Banking is a technology business now, and will become even more so.

Big companies want to know how they can integrate their financial processes with technology, and consumers want quick, responsive, secure, user-friendly applications that get the job done 24/7.

Today you cannot understand or sell finance without understanding technology.

Put time aside each week to start learning digital finance, increase your awareness, increase your knowledge, get involved in projects, and practice learning on the job in the real world to improve your technical skills and appreciation.

Cloud computing

Cloud computing is the delivery of computing services such as servers, storage, databases, networking, analytics and more over the internet. Cloud providers typically charge for these services based on usage, similar to your electricity or gas supplier. Major providers of cloud computing services for large enterprises include Alibaba, Amazon, Microsoft and Oracle. Google's G-Suite cloud platform allows users to

collaborate in real time with applications such as Gmail, Docs, Drive, Calendar, Video Hangouts, and more.

Many of us are using cloud computing services now without even knowing it. If you're sending emails, watching films, listening to music, storing pictures or playing games online it's likely that cloud computing is making it all possible behind the scenes.

Cloud computing offers tremendous opportunities for banks to revitalize their information technology infrastructure, given the current multitude of different legacy systems across many providers. Cloud computing also offers new market entrants the ability to have tremendous data processing power quickly, and allows them to compete against large incumbents in ways not previously possible.

Many banks are undergoing complete transformation of their systems to cloud-based technologies in order to facilitate faster innovation and improved customer service, and provide real-time capabilities to support new real-time banking systems.

Cloud computing will be a key element to enabling digital transformation for major banks and financial services providers worldwide. Many banks are already well on their cloud computing journey. DBS Group Holdings Ltd of Singapore is one such example of a bank actively pursuing a digital agenda with the support of cloud computing. Formerly known as the Development Bank of Singapore and now rebranded the Digital Bank of Singapore, DBS is embedding digital technology and processes into its business and across employees and customers.

DBS have moved from legacy technology, such as big mainframes in large data centers, to cloud computing–based technology. According to DBS they are using digital technology and innovation to extend their reach, enhance efficiencies and create tomorrow's solutions.

DBS point out in their recent annual report these changes, coupled with increased usage of microservices and open-source applications,

have enabled them to reduce infrastructure costs and at the same time improve resiliency and nimbleness.

Outside of the financial services industry, companies such as Tetra Pak use cloud-connected machines to predict exactly when equipment needs maintenance. Businesses such as AT&T are moving thousands of on-premises databases and terabytes of data to cloud-based systems – in this example the provider is Oracle Cloud.

However, approximately only 5% of global computing is cloud based, presenting amazing opportunities for growth and innovation. Amazon Web Services alone is a US$20 billion revenue run rate business with a runway of growth opportunity before it. Alibaba is also aggressively ramping up its cloud computing offering and revenues.

Many banks are planning to invest to create a single, more scalable and modern data platform through which customer information can be accessed more easily, the goal being to provide customers with personalized experiences based on deeper insight and analysis. Cloud computing systems are likely to provide the answer.

Artificial intelligence

Artificial intelligence is the ability of computer systems to perform tasks normally requiring human intelligence such as visual perception, speech recognition, decision-making and language translation.

Without doubt artificial intelligence is one of the biggest areas of investment for banks, given its ability to radically reshape the front-end customer experience and deliver efficiency in back-end operational activities. Looking to 2020 and beyond, data managed intelligently through artificial intelligence will be a key asset that banks can use innovatively for competitive advantage.

Technology giants such as Microsoft are making great progress building infrastructure such as Microsoft Azure to manage increasing artificial intelligence workloads.

Reports vary on the amount of savings artificial intelligence will deliver for financial services but generally land somewhere between US$1 trillion and US$1.2 trillion.

These savings generally fall into one of three key areas.

- **Front office:** ~US$500 billion in savings through reduction in scale of branch networks, tellers, cashiers and associated security costs.

- **Middle office:** ~US$350 billion through automating compliance activities such as know your customer (KYC) and anti money laundering (AML), and implementing better ways of form processing, data processing and account application management.

- **Back office:** ~US$250 billion through more intelligent fraud management and better funds reconciliation and collection systems.

Already banks are using AI in day-to-day operations to perform a range of activities from transaction monitoring to detection of suspicious activity.

Some key examples of artificial intelligence already working in banking today are:

- chatbots
- document management and analysis
- fraud detection
- machine learning
- robots.

Let's have a look at each of these.

Chatbots

Chatbot conversational interfaces are being deployed by many banks around the world to automate repetitive, high-volume front-office tasks such as credit card general enquiries. These technologies use a natural language to understand what customers are requesting.

HDFC Bank in India use their chatbot 'Eva' to handle customer queries and provide information on products and services. In the first 12 months of operation Eva handled over one million conversations, and is able to respond to simple questions in less than 0.4 seconds.

In South America, Brazilian Bank Bradesco are using artificial intelligence based on IBM's Watson platform to interact with people in natural language and answer questions about products and services based on voice and text commands.

Expect to see many more banking chatbots with exotic names like 'Eva' and 'Bolt' operating through the Facebook Messenger platform over the coming years.

Document management and analysis

JP Morgan have introduced AI-based technology to review data from 12,000 annual credit agreements, which normally takes 360,000 human hours. AI technology is able to analyze thousands of legal documents and extract important data points and clauses in seconds when it previously took thousands of hours.

Fraud detection

Citibank have made a strategic investment in Feedzai, a data science company that focuses in real time on online and in-person banking fraud. Feedzai can scan huge amounts of data to recognize evolving fraud threats and notify customers automatically as these threats emerge.

Machine learning

Machine learning is a subset of artificial intelligence that uses statistical methods to give computers the ability to 'learn'. In other words, to progressively improve performance on a specific task without being specifically programmed.

Machine learning is being deployed across many industries and sectors, with notable examples being Amazon's personal recommendations based on items you have recently purchased.

Voice recognition systems such as Apple Siri and Microsoft Cortana are voice recognition systems that use machine learning to imitate interacting with humans. And Google has been intensively investing in machine learning, and use it to deliver multiple products such as:

- Google Maps to analyze traffic data and send the fastest route in real time to your smartphone

- Google Assistant to manage your verbal request for information

- Google Translate, which quickly converts one language to another.

In financial services, PayPal are using machine learning algorithms and mining of huge volumes of data to evaluate risk and combat fraud.

Many of the auto-reconciliation technologies being offered by banks and third parties to automate accounts receivable data, outstanding invoices and bank statement data information are also based on machine learning technology.

Robots

Retailers such as Amazon already use an army of 45,000 robots in warehouses to help pick, pack and fulfil orders. DIY retailer Lowe's are using robots to lead customers to the paint area in store and to manage inventory.

And – look out – the robot is coming to a bank branch near you. For example, HDFC Bank in India is trialing an intelligent robotic assistant (IRA).

Placed at the front of the branch, the IRA welcomes customers and can answer frequently asked questions. In addition, you can be escorted by the IRA to the appropriate customer service kiosk to deal with your specific enquiry. If you want to enquire about a mortgage, the IRA will lead you to the relevant product specialist to help.

In Shanghai, China Construction Bank are trialing a completely staffless branch managed by technology including robots, artificial intelligence and facial recognition.

OCBC in Singapore are using robotic process automation (RPA) from two robots 'Bob' and 'Zac' to speed up and automate processes. Bob does home loan restructuring work, where previously 199 process

steps were managed by employees toggling across five systems and 27 screens for one application, which took 45 minutes. The process has been reduced to around one minute in total now.

Zac generates sales reports that previously took a human two hours to complete, with the task now being completed in 12 minutes. The process automates 166 process steps and collation of information from multiple spreadsheets, and is now available at 9 am daily instead of previously 4 pm.

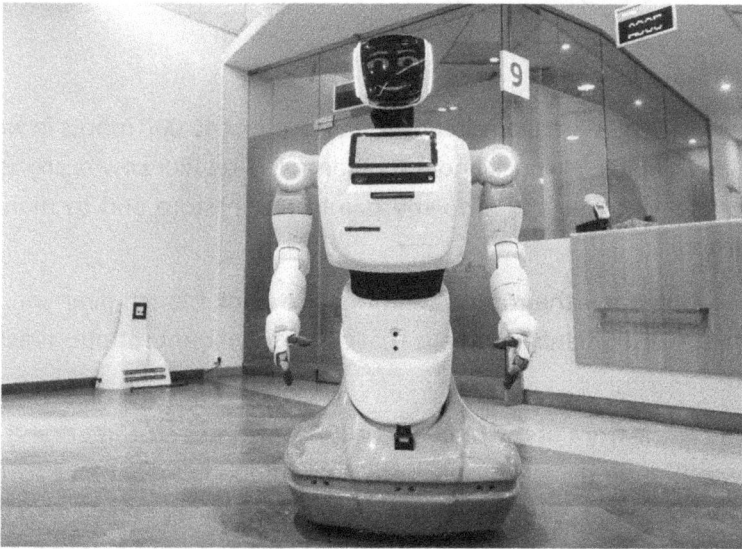

These technologies are fast, efficient, and there is no need for coffee or tea breaks.

Expect to see much wider use of robots and robotic process automation across banking in data-generating and repetitive-task activities where faster speed, better availability, more accuracy and improved compliance checking are required.

The internet of things

IOT – or the internet of things – is a network of smartwatches, smartphones, wearables, connected cars, home appliances and other physical items connected to the internet. Anything from planes, fridges, cars, scales, hairbrushes and other physical items across consumer and industrial devices are collecting and communicating data over the internet.

For example:

- Rolls Royce uses IOT to automatically capture and send information about flight plans, weather, technical statistics and fuel usage back to employees to track possible problems and schedule replacement parts in advance.

- The gym chain Fitness First uses sensors to track who enters their gym facilities based on customer wearables and smartphones.

- Schneider Electric has built a smart farming platform to allow farmers to better manage water use in responsible and sustainable ways. Over 50% of our fresh water is used for agricultural purposes so efficient use is important. Live data from sensors on the farm combined with pricing access from water utility providers allows farmers to maximize crop and livestock yields by using water at the most efficient times.

The IOT evolution also has knock-on impacts to banking, from simple scenarios like users paying from a wearable device such as FitPay to more advanced scenarios. In agriculture, for example, real-time data generated on crops and livestock will allow banking providers and lenders to better monitor the supply chain, yield and land values.

As IOT widely spreads across commercial and retail-related industries, new cases for financial services integration will occur.

Open banking

Open banking is essentially a secure way to give providers access to your financial information.

Through application programming interfaces (APIs), financial institution data is provided to users. An open banking standard defines how financial data should be created, shared and accessed.

Open banking is designed to improve the customer experience in several ways, including forcing larger banks to compete with smaller and newer banks, making the task of switching provider from one bank's account to another's easier. Open banking makes it easier to introduce new tailored apps and products to customers, and allows those same customers to see if they can get a better solution.

Financial consumers are about to see a whole new world of apps and websites using their data to provide tailored offers and niche solutions. You will also be able to see all your money in one place through account aggregation services, a very useful addition if like me you have bank accounts with multiple providers.

Open banking threatens incumbent bank relationships by facilitating increased competition. More than ever, established banks will need to find new ways to manage not only their internal data but how they use that to service, maintain and sell to customers.

Open banking ultimately offers challenges from large fintechs such as Amazon and Google as well as challenger banks looking to exploit the data to their advantage. A great range of other opportunities are also presented, including facilitating banks to better communicate with and understand their existing customers and what is most important to them.

It also offers opportunity to attract new customers and grow existing ones through upselling and cross-selling.

APIs

API is the abbreviation for application programming interface. It is essentially software that allows two applications to talk to each other.

We are using APIs every day without even knowing it. When you search for a flight on a website such as Skyscanner, Kayak or Expedia, the website API's messaging technology essentially communicates with the airlines' systems to bring you pricing and availability. APIs govern how one application can talk with another. For example:

- Businesses can use Google APIs to present mapping and branch location information on their website.

- Facebook APIs offer the ability for ad, game and other app developers to use Facebook as a common log in and provides great ways to quickly engage with a large audience.

In banking, APIs will be a huge growth area over the next few years – the 'API economy' is already being referred to.

For example, APIs offer the ability for companies and developers to work with banks to develop new value-added services, or indeed for fintech entrepreneurs to develop their own innovative API solutions.

Other developments in this area include:

- Many banks, including BBVA and Citibank, now offer API sandboxes where developers can build, develop and test new financial APIs.

- Citibank use API-driven connectivity to allow their institutional clients to connect across 96 countries using the client's own Treasury and Enterprise Resource Planning (ERP) system technologies to manage payments and receipts.

- JP Morgan has an API store to allow businesses and merchants to easily integrate with the bank's services.

- DBS Bank in Singapore's API platform has over 180 applications across more than 60 partners at the time of writing, and this number is increasing.

APIs will also come forward in financial services in two distinct forms – Commercial APIs and Open Banking APIs:

- Commercial APIs are commercial applications developed by or for a specific use to a bank's target customer base.

- Open Banking APIs will allow start-ups and developers to build a new wave of applications, systems and platforms for managing finances that can be deployed across multiple providers.

An industry-standard level of information will be available on which to develop products such as account balance, spend history and outgoing payments.

As open banking arrives in more markets, look out for a sharp increase in new attractive payment channels, different ways of obtaining credit and loans, and completely new developments in savings and investment management, many of which will be based on API technology.

Apps

An app is a computer program that is designed for use on a mobile digital device, and we are all familiar with how they are filling up our mobile phone screens and how we are relying on them more and more. Whether it be Google Maps, Facebook, WhatsApp, YouTube, Instagram, Messenger or the new TikTok in China, you will be interacting with apps to run your daily life now.

In banking you will probably be using your bank's app to make payments on the move and check account balances. However, there is a

new wave of banking apps coming to consumers offering rich functionality and great features.

Revolut is an intuitive app that allows you to open a bank account within minutes. It offers real rate currency exchange, free debit card and chargeless transactions in 130 currencies and ability to purchase cryptocurrencies as innovative and new features.

N26 offers every certified user a free bank account with Maestro or Mastercard. The app uses TransferWise to provide low-cost money transfers and also MoneyBeam instant payments and Apple Pay integration.

Banks are ferociously competing to try to match the speed and innovation of new entrants like Revolut and N26, and ensure their app and offering is good enough to win and retain customers. For sure the app will be an important part of the banking sales proposition moving forward.

Social payments

Social payment is the use of social media to transfer money to another person or business. The early innovator was Paypal, and subsequently many others have emerged and are emerging such as Venmo, Snapcash, Google Wallet, Apple Pay and Twitter Buy.

It is money in a message, and just like a message we want to do it now.

Similar to WhatsApp or WeChat, you establish peer-to-peer communication with a friend or family member using your mobile phone – as long as both people have the app the sender can initiate social money transfer.

With the tremendous growth of social media apps for communication and the reduction of cash usage worldwide, social payments are set

to experience tremendous growth over the coming years. These social networks and messaging providers have huge potential to dislocate financial services over the coming years. It's happening already, with WhatsApp pay services beta testing in India and working with banks such as ABSA in South Africa. And the parent company of WhatsApp, Facebook, have a payments license in Europe now, so look out for further developments in that region.

Amazon Banking already has approximately 500,000 customers in India, a market with huge growth potential. ICICI Bank of India is partnering with Paytm, Google Tez and WhatsApp to offer its customers cashless payments in this market. WhatsApp alone has around 200 million users in India, so the growth potential is significant.

Money as a message is really set to take off towards 2020 and beyond, with new entrants coming to challenge early innovators. For example, Kakao (Korea), Go-Jek (Indonesia), Grab (Asia) and WeChat Pay in China are likely to see fresh competition coming from the large fintechs and established social platforms.

Facial recognition

Facial recognition systems are capable of identifying or verifying a person from a digital image or video frame or source.

With more cases of facial recognition systems coming into our daily lives at airport security, in cities through closed circuit TV (CCTV) surveillance and building access control, expect to see a new wave of facial recognition technology emerging where it will rapidly move from the security industries to banking and finance. For example, HSBC business customers are able to log into their HSBCnet mobile application with just their face. Quick, secure, convenient, and no need to remember passwords.

Many other banks are launching apps with facial recognition log-in capabilities. In the UK alone providers including Royal Bank of Scotland, First Direct, Halifax and Tesco Bank are among the first to leverage the new iPhone facial recognition software. And Mastercard's 'selfie pay' can allow users to approve online payments by simply showing their face to the smartphone camera.

Moving forward, facial recognition technology will not even require customers to use their credit cards or mobile phones to make payments. In China, Alibaba's Ant Financial is trialing 'smile to pay' in Hangzhou with KFC, where you can buy a Zinger burger and fries by flashing a smile.

We may have to be careful smiling too much in the pub in future years – we may be accidentally buying everyone a round of drinks.

Video in banking

As well as facial recognition for customers logging into banking platforms and approving payments, video use is set to dramatically increase in banking:

- Internal communications and team meetings across video channels such as Zoom, Skype, FaceTime and Google Hangouts will become much more popular as more bank staff work virtually.

- More interactions will take place with customers through video, with video customer meetings becoming commonplace.

- As self-service technologies move transactional processing away from the counter and human involvement, video banking will become very important for the remaining situations that require human interaction and one-on-one support.

For example, Santander in the UK is rolling out video technology across its branches to connect customers to mortgage application specialists based in another location.

- In China, where there is a large rural population, video banking has helped connect farmers and rural employees to services and support previously not available without a long trip to a bigger city.

We can expect to see more use of video banking moving forward as it offers benefits to banks and consumers. Video tellers allow banks to reduce costs and have staff working from their homes or satellite offices. For consumers, a wider range of services can be available in their local area or from home. One key issue will be if we can convince an ageing population to embrace such technologies broadly.

Blockchain

Blockchain is an incorruptible ledger of transactions that can have a massive impact on the financial services world. Vitalik Buterin, inventor of Ethereum, feels there is tremendous potential firstly in emerging markets:

> Blockchain solves the problem of manipulation. When I speak about it in the West, people say they trust Google, Facebook, or their banks. But the rest of the world doesn't trust organizations and corporations that much – I mean Africa, India, Eastern Europe, or Russia. It's not about the places where people are really rich. Blockchain's opportunities are the highest in the countries that haven't reached that level yet.

Blockchain offers the ability to bypass a traditional intermediary – the bank or card processor – to deliver person-to-person, peer-to-peer transactions. This technology will have potentially huge impacts on financial services, including common areas such as international payments.

The World Bank estimates that over US$430 billion in money transfers were sent in 2015, a number which is starting to move to upcoming new payment transfer entrants, and over time may well move to blockchain.

Brad Garlinghouse, CEO of Ripple Labs, took the stage at the Money 20/20 Asia Conference in Singapore in March 2018 to explain the World Bank have indicated profit margins on global remittances are currently 7.2%, with a goal to reduce this figure to 3% by 2030. Brad argued that Ripple will have failed as a company if the margin figure is not 30Bps by then. Add to this the fact that between US$10 trillion and US$30 trillion is stuck in the global banking vostro/nostro network at any one time and the case for immediate low-cost transfers and reconciliation becomes clear.

If you can validate me and I can validate you, why do we need a financial intermediary?

Citibank recently partnered with Nasdaq to announce a banking integration that enabled straight-through payment processing and reconciliation by using a distributed ledger to record and transmit payment instructions.

Many banks are exploring blockchain-distributed technologies and smart contracts between parties to improve trade finance where processes are highly paper based, manual, time consuming and costly.

Blockchain also opens up potential changes to identity and data storage, with potential new solutions on who will own and govern our data in the future rather than LinkedIn, Google or Facebook doing it for

us. The data being generated by us is becoming incredibly valuable, so why don't we own and control it? Dock.io is one such blockchain-based venture aiming at putting the user in control of their own data and facilitating sharing in a user-controlled and connected manner.

Look out for blockchain-based technologies moving from proof of concept to more widely adopted technologies across the industry as we move into the 2020s.

Self-driving cars

I spent years on the road in the UK and Australia visiting clients and prospects in my account management and new business acquisition roles. Planning your time effectively and planning routes carefully are indeed some of the key characteristics of effective financial service sales managers.

When client meetings are not taking place over video in the future – for example, in complex situations such as syndicated debt presentations and multi-person transaction banking implementation discussions – there is a high chance a driverless car will be taking you to the appointment.

The amount of time this will free up for people in financial services will be astounding. In the 1990s I often spent 20 to 25 hours a week on the road in the UK (most of that on the M25 motorway). Imagine the extra productivity you would generate if that time could be used for further client prospecting research, preparing for upcoming meetings, completing video meetings, planning ways to grow existing clients and win more new ones.

Waymo, Google's self-driving car company, continues to progress the development and testing of its self-driving technology with a fleet of vehicles in Phoenix, US driving without a person behind the wheel.

Additional machine-learning capabilities also help self-driving cars to better respond to others on the road. As at July 2018, Waymo has achieved eight million miles driven in self-driving cars, double the four million miles driven on public roads from just nine months before in November 2017.

Self-driving cars are definitely coming, and financial services employees will be moving around in them.

Spin offs and side bets

Like many of the technology leaders, many banks and financial services companies will start to develop spin offs and side bets in new ventures as the world continues to move rapidly. Google is already doing this; in fact, their founders expect to make 'smaller bets in areas that might seem very speculative or even strange when compared to our current businesses'. Other example are:

- Standard Chartered Bank has set up a new unit SC Ventures aimed at promoting innovation within their bank. The goal is to invest in disruptive technologies with a professional investment unit to manage minority investments in fintech companies.

- OCBC bank in Singapore have developed the Open Vault project to drive collaboration with external fintech companies and their own innovation unit.

- Spanish bank BBVA has been proactively developing fintech partnerships and has acquired several companies, including Openpay, the Mexican start-up that offers advanced payments solutions and online capabilities for businesses. They have also acquired Holvi, an online bank for entrepreneurs offering digital invoicing and expense management.

- Danske Bank's mobile payment platform, MobilePay, became a separate business entity in 2017 following the launch of their new partnership model, with almost all Danish banks joining the MobilePay partnership. MobilePay remains the most popular mobile payment solution in Denmark and Finland, and remains an important part of their customer offering.

Expect to see further acquisitions across the industry moving forward, and lots of spin offs and side bets in financial services.

Long-term thinking

More and more in the future, despite our always-on, real-time information lifestyle, there will be a move to long-term thinking instead of focusing on the next quarterly earnings report or annual sales targets. Companies are starting to leverage this way of thinking now for their competitive advantage in the fields of banking and technology:

- Amazon still believes it's always 'Day One', and has a relentless focus on four strategic pillars of customer centricity, continuous optimization, culture of innovation and corporate agility. They aspire to be Earth's most customer-centric company, but recognize achieving this will be no small or easy challenge.

- JP Morgan do not worry about their stock price in the short run and do not worry about quarterly earnings. Their mindset is to consistently build the company knowing if they do the right things the stock price will take care of itself.

- Google have clearly stated they will not shy away from high-risk, high-reward projects that they believe are key to their long-term success.

- Bank Bradesco, one of the biggest banks in Brazil, has long-term stock option plans for senior personnel that do not allow them to sell shares in the short term but only when they end their careers with the bank. The founder's original thinking was this focused on long-term planning, long-term results and long-term sustainable growth and share appreciation.

Look out for longer term thinking from industry participants and a renewed focus on their purpose and their 'why'.

CONCLUSION

The banks and bankers of the future will be working virtually, supporting staffless branches, moving around in driverless cars and obtaining real-time analytics yet thinking long term.

They will be supported by their own virtual assistants and work alongside new digital colleagues, with most interactions taking place over video.

Successful banks and employees will be the ones that focus squarely around rapidly evolving customer expectations for both their online and offline requirements.

Some individuals and companies will thrive, some will fail, many will exit the industry and many will also join the industry.

Businesses and individuals in financial services will need to respond to a range of non-traditional competitors looking at new ways of capturing their share of the growing US$2 trillion pie, fueled by economic growth and wealth equalization with niche solutions, new technologies and propositions based on different demographic customer segments.

In this new environment there will be challenges and opportunities for all.

I wish you and your business every success for the future in a world where some will retreat to a world of low revenues and declining customers and some will grow and transform.

DATA SOURCES

IBISWorld Global Commercial Banking Report.

United Nations Conference on Trade and Development.

Global Economy and Development at Brookings, 'The Unprecedented Expansion of the Middle Class', 2017.

EY Fintech Adoption Index 2017, EYGM Limited.

Appendix:
Competitive strategies

This appendix continues from the tables in chapter 1, and looks at the strategies of major banks in all corners of the world. It is designed to give you an idea of key global emerging themes and competitive strategies.

Annual revenue figures are from Yahoo Finance and/or the Company annual report.

Australia

The commercial banking market in Australia is worth an annual A$146 billion according to IBISWorld. Four dominant banks – ANZ, CBA, NAB and Westpac – account for the majority of market share. Other foreign banks active in the market include JP Morgan, Citi, HSBC and BTMU, with combined foreign bank revenues of another A$18 billion generated in Australia. The Australian Government is becoming more supportive of introducing competition to the sector following the recent Royal Banking Commission review, with a new wave of neo-banks and fintech start-ups entering the market. Xinja, Volt and 86,400 are three such new entrants, as are Society One, RateSetter and Prospa in lending. The New South Wales Government is investing heavily in new enterprises, small business, fintech and entrepreneurs with the goal of making Sydney an important fintech hub within Australia and more broadly in Asia.

Bank	Total revenue (billion)	Strategy	Focus	Interesting consideration	Interesting challenge
ANZ	A$19.14	Being the best bank for people who want to buy and own a home, or start, run and grow a small business in Australia and New Zealand. Also, a focus on people moving goods around Asia Pacific.	A focus on becoming a simpler, better balanced and more service-oriented bank.	First bank in market to collaborate with competitive fintech providers as demonstrated by offering the Apple Pay service to cardholders.	Embedding a purpose- and values-led transformation.
Commonwealth Bank	A$24.82	Strong application of technology combined with strong customer focus.	Building a stronger institutional business and developing select offshore capabilities.	Managing a large mortgage portfolio where Australians have their highest ever debt levels compared to salaries.	Maintaining number one customer satisfaction service scores in retail business.
NAB	A$18.31	To become Australia and New Zealand's most respected bank. Strong focus on business bank mid-sized customers.	Focusing on priority areas of home owners and investors. Within the business banking market, small and medium business customers remain a priority.	Managing environment where some households' and businesses' stagnant wage growth, coupled with consumer caution, is causing some concerns.	Embedding agile practices to redesign customers' end-to-end experiences across products.

Bank	Total revenue (billion)	Strategy	Focus	Interesting consideration	Interesting challenge
Westpac	A$21.42	To be one of the world's great service companies with a focus across five pillars of performance disciplines, service leadership, digital transformation, targeted growth, and workforce revolution.	Strong focus on Australian mortgages.	Tightening of credit standards and limits related to mortgage may lead to slower growth in lending. Maintaining position as world's most sustainable bank.	Managing five distinct bank brands within the group: Westpac, St George, Bank of Melbourne, Bank SA and RAMS.

UK

The UK commercial banking industry is worth some GBP126 billion in revenues. Barclays, HSBC, Lloyds Banking Group and Royal Bank of Scotland are the dominant providers in this market, accounting for over GBP80 billion of market revenues or approximately 65%.

Bank	Total revenue (billion)	Strategy	Focus	Interesting consideration	Interesting challenge
Barclays	GBP18.92	Focus on transatlantic consumers and wholesale banking across UK and US markets.	Migration from restructuring focus to digital thinking and shareholder focus.	Preparing for Brexit changes, which includes setting up a new 'ring-fenced' bank for 24 million customers and transferring them.	In middle of one of banking's biggest ever restructures resulting in an 80,000 staff reduction. Currently exiting operations in Africa.
HSBC	US$49.62	Connecting international trade and capital flows and focusing on wealth creation around demographic changes.	Seeking to capitalize on global demographic trends such as increasing global trade, emerging market expansion, growing middle class in Asia and climate change renewables investments.	Have achieved a US$338 billion reduction in risk-weighted assets.	Finalizing a group-wide transformation focused on resizing and simplifying the business and redeploying capital in growth areas.
Lloyds Bank	GBP17.51	Focus on helping Britain prosper. GBP6 billion of new lending assigned for start-ups, SMEs and mid-market customers.	Focus on leading customer experience through digitization, work transformation and training, and aligning group-wide capabilities.	Managing one of UK's largest branch networks with over 1,000 branches.	Major modernization of IT infrastructure and data management under way.

Bank	Total revenue (billion)	Strategy	Focus	Interesting consideration	Interesting challenge
Royal Bank of Scotland	GBP12.66	Aiming to become number one for customer service, trust and advocacy with their customers. Also working on becoming a simpler, safer, more focused bank.	Have introduced a new video banking service that lets customers chat face-to-face with a personal banker.	Grappling with uncertainty of how the UK leaves the EU and an economy growing below the 2% long-run average.	Aiming to potentially restart privatization from the UK Treasury by end of March 2019.

Canada

Bank of Montreal, Canadian Imperial Bank of Commerce, Royal Bank of Canada, Toronto–Dominion Bank and Scotiabank are the big five dominant banks in Canada, and are currently responsible for managing over 75% of the country's banking revenues.

Bank	Total revenue (billion)	Strategy	Focus	Interesting consideration	Interesting challenge
Bank of Montreal	C$22.37	Strong focus on listening to the customer and reinvesting in technology for customer service improvements.	Focus on Canadian consumers and businesses and development in six US Midwest states.	Managing moderating growth in consumer spending resulting from two 2017 central bank interest rate hikes and elevated household debt.	Managing an expanding American business.
Canadian Imperial Bank of Commerce	C$16.96	Focus on clients, innovation and expansion into US market.	Expansion into US private wealth market as demonstrated through acquisition of Geneva Advisors.	More than 40 leaders across the bank changed responsibilities with the goal of cross-pollinating ideas across the business and strengthening the team.	Embedding the 2017 acquisition of US bank The PrivateBank.
Royal Bank of Canada	C$41.26	Maintain focus in Canadian domestic custody, asset services and cash management. Goal to increase current client acquisition up to three times, leading to 2.5 million new clients by 2023.	Focus on corporate, institutional and high-net-worth clients in the US.	Managing rapidly changing customer expectations, changing technology landscape and regulatory environment.	Maintain number one market position and strong deposit and payment business.

BANKING 2020 (page 138)

Bank	Total revenue (billion)	Strategy	Focus	Interesting consideration	Interesting challenge
Toronto–Dominion Bank	C$36.35	Thinking like a customer and owner and executing efficiently.	Focus on Canadian retail, US retail, and wholesale banking.	Managing business in an environment where households have been slowing their spending to a more sustainable rate. In addition, government measures to cool house price growth and support long-term financial stability are key considerations for future lending.	Embedding the 2017 Scotttrade acquisition.
Scotiabank	C$26.16	Renewed customer focus, digital transformation, leadership investment, cost transformation and business mix management.	Ongoing focus on Pacific Alliance region which comprises Mexico, Peru, Chile and Colombia.	Setting up and embedding digital factories across geographical markets.	Effectively managing the business where over 50,000 of 88,000 staff reside outside of Canada.

Germany

As the largest economy in Europe, Germany has a large commercial banking system generating Euro 61 billion in annual revenues. While the country's banks support domestic consumers and businesses, they are also heavily invested in supporting German manufacturers exporting abroad.

CommerzBank AG, Deutsche Bank AG and HVB Group are the dominant providers in this market, accounting for approximately 70% of market share.

Also listed here are Dutch Bank ING who are making good progress on their digital strategy and global expansion.

Bank	Total revenue (billion)	Strategy	Focus	Interesting consideration	Interesting challenge
Commerzbank	E8.5 billion	Strong focus on the Mittelstand, German business small business customer. Goal of being simple, digital and efficient.	Commerzbank 4.0 development focused on focused growth, digitization and efficiency.	Carefully managing staff restructuring program underway. Also managing Brexit situation carefully where 550,000 jobs in Germany are dependent on exports to the UK.	Working hard to digitize 80% of business processes by 2020.
Deutsche Bank	E25.92	Goal to be simpler and more efficient, less risky, better capitalized and better run with more disciplined execution.	Maintain strong focus on corporate and investment banking.	Managing any risks associated with UK exit from the European union.	Managing the sale of Concardis payment processing and stake in PCC business in Poland. Spin off of Deutsche Asset Management (Deutsche AM) being planned on Frankfurt stock exchange.
DZ Bank	E6.52	Focused on supporting 900 local and cooperative banks across Germany.	Focus on insurance, home savings, and personal investment products.	Managing large local cooperative bank network in increasingly fast-moving technical age.	Managing structural merger of DG Hyp Bank and WL Bank.

Bank	Total revenue (billion)	Strategy	Focus	Interesting consideration	Interesting challenge
ING Bank	E16.97	Build a scalable digital banking platform across borders that provides customers with the same clear and easy experience. Earn the primary relationship, develop analytics skills to understand customers better, increase the pace of innovation to serve changing customer needs, think beyond traditional banking to develop new services and business models.	Executing Think Forward strategy to empower people to stay a step ahead in life and in business.	Managing ING Ventures fund to invest in start-ups and companies that have already gained some market traction.	Managing increasing regulation and regulatory costs in face of growing fintech competition.

France

Two of the largest 10 banks in the world by assets are French, with BNP Paribas and Crédit Agricole significant global players. As the world economy strengthens these banks are likely to play a significant role globally moving forward.

Bank	Total revenue (billion)	Strategy	Focus	Interesting consideration	Interesting challenge
BNP Paribas	E40.74	Accelerating transformation in order to be the European bank of reference.	Strong focus on retail banking in France, Belgium, Italy and Luxembourg. Corporate and institutional banking also has global focus and generates 29% of group revenues.	Building a business that delivers the group values of agility, client satisfaction, compliance culture and openness.	Managing 2020 Digital Transformation Plan.
Crédit Agricole	E32.10	Building the 2020 strategic ambition comprising a digital revolution, strengthening core business lines, improving operational efficiency and embedding new ownership structure.	Building a multi-channel bank that is 100% human and 100% digital.	Managing business in face of multi-faceted competition from aggregators, neobanks, fintech, insure tech and big technology companies such as Google, Amazon, Facebook and Apple.	Managing growing number of global, European Union and national regulations as well other market standards.
Société Générale	E24.75	Implement the Transform to Grow 2020 strategic plan comprising fostering responsibility, further refocus, transformation, delivering on costs and growing.	Realize additional growth from investments in Russian and African markets.	Exiting non-synergetic markets such as Albania and private banking in Belgium.	Managing environment where European banking is facing deep and long-term transformation.

Bank	Total revenue (billion)	Strategy	Focus	Interesting consideration	Interesting challenge
BPCE	£22.76	Focus on three main business divisions: retail banking and insurance, asset and wealth management, and corporate and investment banking.	2020 digital transformation program with £600 million invested per year.	Managing group structure which includes 14 cooperative banks.	Strong focus on being a bancassurance specialist.

South America

Bank	Total revenue (billion)	Strategy	Focus	Interesting consideration	Interesting challenge
Banco De Brasil	BRL 24.7 (US$6.58)	Focus on Brazilian individual, commercial and banking markets. Some offshore presence for permanent resident use and international Brazilian companies.	Focusing more on digital transformation strategy.	Important to have acceleration in economy again to drive growth of loan portfolio, especially to individuals.	Controlled by the Brazilian Government but need to identify innovations in the finance and technology sectors and anticipating trends to ensure longevity. Renewed investment in cyber and information security.
Bancolombia	COP11.14 (~US$3.55)	Focus on client experience, innovation, humanistic culture, sustainable profitability and technical excellency.	Strong focus on domestic commercial banking.	Big focus on environment and sustainability through paper saving, car sharing and other internal initiatives.	Transition to a more technological-based enterprise.

Bank	Total revenue (billion)	Strategy	Focus	Interesting consideration	Interesting challenge
Banco de Chile	CLP1438 (~US$2.15)	Customer centricity, efficiency and sustainability through collaboration and committed to Chilean development.	Maintain diversified business model across wholesale and retail customers. Overlay with customer focus and digital focus.	Embedding a new CRM system and building digital transformation capabilities.	Managing business in an environment of sluggish economic growth, higher corporate tax rates and a sharp rise in competition.
Banorte Mexico	MXN66 (~US$3.45)	Focus on strong Mexicans and a strong Mexico.	Building out strategic alliance signed with PayPal in October 2017 to help Mexicans make payments onshore and offshore from linked accounts and credit cards.	Renegotiation of NAFTA free trade agreement to take place between Mexico and US Government. The present agreement has helped Mexico significantly develop.	Helping the country recover from two devastating earthquakes in 2017.

Middle East

Bank	Total revenue (billion)	Strategy	Growth strategies	Interesting market consideration	Interesting challenge
Qatar National Bank	QAR21.05 (US$5.78)	Focus on four primary areas: utilities, transport, 2022 FIFA World Cup® infrastructure, and real estate.	Focus on Middle East, Africa and South East Asia.	Maintaining number one bank position in Qatar and expanding international diversification. Supporting Qatar's vision to become a knowledge-based and diversified economy by 2030.	Carefully assessing global leverage and impacts of low oil price era.
National Commercial Bank Saudi Arabia	SAR 16.41 (~US$4.37)	Goal to become region's premier financial services group based on number one in revenues, number one in profit, best in customer service, best digital bank, and employer of choice.	Strong focus on SME financing and national infrastructure projects.	Managing environment with subdued oil prices and a sharp fall in the returns on global bonds.	Plans to support significant national large-scale projects such as privatization programs, construction of airports, the Neom Cross-Border Project and the Red Sea Project.

Bank	Total revenue (billion)	Strategy	Growth strategies	Interesting market consideration	Interesting challenge
Isbank Turkey	Total operating income 16,577,658 Turkish Lira TL (~US$3.4 billion)	To be most preferred provider in all sectors and groups operating in Turkey.	Core focus on being Turkey's best digital bank.	Keep supporting all sectors of Turkish economy collectively growing over 7% in 2017.	Maintaining strong support for SME sector.
Emirates NBD	AED 15,455 (~US$4.21)	Embed renovated branches that are more digitally enabled to make them more service focused, in line with 'high-touch high-tech' philosophy.	Expanding international network in India, Egypt and Saudi Arabia.	Manage environment with lower oil prices which affects regional government budgets and drives revenue diversification.	Preparing for a strong and important Expo 2020 in Dubai.
Bank Hapoalim Israel	NIS14.3 (US$3.88)	Deeper connections in target customer segments, value enhancement through personal, human and technological connections and building tomorrow's infrastructure.	Targeting development of international operations including Turkey and continued operational excellence.	Continue supporting the majority of Israel's high-growth technology sector.	Managing the fast pace of global technological change and competition.

India

The world's second most populous nation has huge opportunities for financial services providers. With a population of 1.355 billion and a mix of digital savvy and rural-based consumers, banking and technology providers with innovative solutions can reach farmers in remote areas and customers who were previously unbanked and cash dependent.

Bank	Total revenue (billion)	Strategy	Focus	Interesting consideration	Interesting challenge
State Bank of India	INR839 (~US$11.9)	Supporting India's transformation.	Expanded role out of 'YONO' (You Only Need One) omnichannel banking app.	Managing very large branch network of 22,414 branches.	Managing high expectations from a more digitally savvy customer base.
ICICI Bank	INR667 (~US$9.4)	Strong focus on supporting rural India digitally.	Further rollout of mobile payments, including iMobile and Eazypay mobile application for merchants to collect payments and the 'Mera iMobile' mobile application for rural customers.	Expanding on the boost in digital payments generated from the government's withdrawal of 500 and 1,000 value notes in 2017.	Expanding ICICI Foundation which undertook an initiative of transforming 100 villages into 'ICICI Digital Villages'.
HDFC Bank	INR523.9 (~US$7.4)	Philosophy based on five key areas of: Customer Focus, Operational Excellence, Product Leadership, People and Sustainability.	Supporting farmers, the backbone of the country's economy, as well as microfinance and small business loans.	Supporting local needs of farmers based in diverse agro-climatic zones across India.	Maintaining strong focus on automobile lending.
Bank of Baroda	INR92.2 (~US$1.3)	Transform and grow 'core' business units in retail, corporate, SME, agri and international while carefully managing stressed assets.	Supporting the unbanked and making farmers financially literate. Expanding portable branches.	Continuing transformation program to deal with the legacy of bad loans and to create a modern and competitive bank.	Expanding financing to farmer producer companies in a tie up with SFAC (Small Farmers' Agribusiness Consortium).

ACKNOWLEDGEMENTS

I'd like to thank the team at Dent Global for setting me on the course to write this book in the first place. To Lucy McCarraher at Rethink Press for her guidance and expertise in guiding me through writing this book. Michael Hanrahan at MH Publishing for his unwavering support and expertise in getting the book published.

For American Express and in particular David Thomas and Harry Richmond for giving me my first chance in financial services sales. I was green but hungry to learn, a dangerous combination when looking back on my career. To Gavin Toole for backing me to deliver results for ANZ Institutional Banking.

To all the colleagues and lifetime friends I have met through my career too numerous to mention.

To my beautiful partner Jessica who has supported me constantly through the highs and lows and through no sales and no sleep.

To my Mother (Valerie) and Father (Terry) for always believing in me and supporting my goals and dreams.

I hope anyone reading the book learns something interesting you can use to increase your sales in the world of global financial services. Remember to constantly change and transform and focus on the customer not on the sale as we race towards 2020 and beyond.

ABOUT MARK SWAIN

Mark Swain is a banking business advisor and fintech investor with over 25 years of financial services, payments and strategic sales experience at executive level with companies such as American Express, ANZ Bank and Ingram Micro. His international banking sales career spawned $10 billion in new transaction values mandated, and over $100 million of profits won in the financial services and technology industries.

During his career he developed the TRANSFORM sales methodology, which helped him consistently deliver sales out-performance and also assisted in launching and growing his own successful tech start-up in the UK.

After a successful career, he now spends the majority of his time providing strategic sales growth advice and employee training to financial services businesses and is involved in a variety of banking start-ups.

Mark is deeply passionate about the combination of customer focus, sales process discipline and innovation in financial services to create opportunities for the unbanked and underprivileged and the businesses that serve them.

His financial services TRANSFORM sales methodology is available at www.nosalesnosleep.com and he can be contacted through www.markswain.com.au

Additional copies of this book can be obtained through www.banking2020book.com

www.ingramcontent.com/pod-product-compliance
Lightning Source LLC
Chambersburg PA
CBHW070729220326
41598CB00024BA/3359